GURUS ON E-BUSINESS

JOHN MIDDLETON

Viva Books

New Delhi | Mumbai | Chennai | Kolkata | Bangalore | Hyderabad | Kochi | Guwahati

First Indian Edition 2007
Reprinted 2008, 2010

VIVA BOOKS PRIVATE LIMITED

- 4737/23 Ansari Road, Daryaganj, New Delhi 110 002
E-mail: vivadelhi@vivagroupindia.net, Tel. 42242200
- 76, Service Industries, Shirvane, Sector 1, Nerul, Navi Mumbai 400 706
E-mail: vivamumbai@vivagroupindia.net, Tel. 27721273, 27721274
- Jamals Fazal Chambers, 26 Greams Road, Chennai 600 006
E-mail: vivachennai@vivagroupindia.net, Tel. 28290304, 28294241
- B-103, Jindal Towers, 21/1A/3 Darga Road, Kolkata 700 017
E-mail: vivakolkata@vivagroupindia.net, Tel. 22836381, 22816713
- 7, Sovereign Park Apartments, 56-58, K. R. Road, Basavanagudi, Bangalore 560 004
E-mail: vivabangalore@vivagroupindia.net, Tel. 26607409, 26607410
- 101-102 Mughal Marc Apartments, 3-4-637 to 641, Narayanguda, Hyderabad 500 029
E-mail: vivahyderabad@vivagroupindia.net, Tel. 27564481, 27564482
- Beevi Towers, First Floor, SRM Road, Kaloor, Kochi 682 018, Kerala
E-mail: vivakochi@vivagroupindia.net, Tel: 0484-2403055, 2403056
- 232, GNB Road, Beside UCO Bank, Silpukhuri, Guwahati 781 003
E-mail: vivaguwahati@vivagroupindia.net, Tel: 0361-2666386

www.vivagroupindia.com

Published by arrangement with

Thorogood Publishers Limited
10-12 Rivington Street
London EC2A 3DU,
UK

ISBN: 978-81-309-0699-7

Published by Vinod Vasishtha for Viva Books Private Limited, 4737/23, Ansari Road, Daryaganj, New Delhi-110 002. Printed and bound by Sanat Printers, Kundli - 131 028.

The author

John Middleton is Co-Director of the Centre for Strategic Thinking, a membership-based organization that exists to promote better quality thinking and planning practices within UK companies. Recognized as a leading expert in decision-making tools and processes, he specializes in working with individuals and organizations that are determined to make best use of the future.

From 1996 until 2004, he was Director of the Bristol Management Research Centre, before which he spent 18 years working for BAA (formerly the British Airports Authority) and AXA Sun Life in various senior HR roles, covering recruitment, training, management development, information systems and HR strategy.

John is a Chartered Member of the Institute of Personnel and Development, as well as a member of the Institute of Directors.

He holds a Masters Degree from the University of Bristol, where he has been an Associate Lecturer since 1994. He has taught IT Management on Manchester Business School's International MBA programme since 2001.

He has written 11 books to date, including *Writing the New Economy* (Capstone, 2000), *The Ultimate Strategy Library* (Capstone, 2003), *Culture* (Capstone, 2002), and *Upgrade Your Brain* (Infinite Ideas, 2006)

From 1996 to 2002, he published and edited *Future Filter*, a bi-monthly business digest covering trends and developments in the new economy.

His email address is john.middleton@mac.com

Contents

Acknowledgements

I would like to thank

The 'Friends of e-Business' – colleagues, acquaintances and chums – whose advice, tips, and comments about which e-business gurus should be featured here (and, just as crucially, who in their view didn't merit a place) helped me to end up with a final list that was a vast improvement over my initial attempt. The final decision though about what went in was mine, so I alone deserve it on the chin for any howlers, omissions, or glaring errors of judgment.

My fellow Co-Director at the Centre for Strategic Thinking Bob Gorzynski, whose regular pearls of wisdom have enhanced my understanding of business strategy and of the e-business environment.

Finally, I could not have written this book without the support of my wife Julie, particularly in the final days of writing. Thanks also to our children Guy and Helena who, if they ever think about e-business when they are older and forging their own careers, will probably wonder what all the fuss was about. To you all with love.

The scope of this book

This book explores the impact and significance of e-business as illustrated by the work and thinking of a number of key players in the field. Its aim is to be an accessible guide aimed at business people who are looking to make optimal and profitable use of e-business, as well as at students and others who are looking for a deeper understanding of the subject.

Introduction

We thought the creation and operation of websites was mysterious Nobel prize stuff, the province of the wild-eyed and purple-haired. Any company, old or new, that does not see this technology as important as breathing could be on its last breath.

JACK WELCH, FORMER CHAIRMAN OF GENERAL ELECTRIC, QUOTED IN THE OBSERVER, 14TH MAY 2000

In truth, we have never experienced anything quite like the internet. Other great transformative technologies – railways, electricity, the telephone, the motor car, and so on – took decades to achieve the level of impact that the internet has achieved in just a handful of years.

The new information technologies that brought countless dot.com businesses into being have created a global market place, restructured whole industry sectors, challenged conventional economic thinking, redefined how business is done, and impacted to varying degrees on every worker on the planet.

Peter Drucker, as ever, has captured this phenomenon in a few choice words: 'The traditional factors of production – land, labour and capital – are becoming restraints rather than driving forces... Knowledge has become the central, key resource that knows no geography. It underlies the most significant and unprecedented social phenomenon of this century. No class in history has ever risen as fast as the blue-collar worker and no class has ever fallen as fast. All within less than a century'.

This unprecedented speed of change has inevitably led to organizations having to learn on the hoof, with little time possible for considered reflection. The result has been organizational carnage, with a huge increase in the number of job losses and business failures over the past few years. For many organizations, the internet has proved to be more of a graveyard than a gravy train.

The influence of technology

Here are just a few of the ways in which technology has changed the way that organizations and their people work:

Instant global news, instant global impact

News, ideas and information travels faster. Profits at investment banks, airlines, and the wider tourist industry collapsed in the immediate aftermath of America's terrorist attacks. Lay-offs and job cuts followed rapidly.

Geography matters less

Location is becoming a less important factor in business decision-making. Companies are locating screen-based activity wherever they find the best deal in terms of skills and productivity. Developing countries increasingly perform on-line services – running call centres, writing software, and so on.

Nine to five becomes 24/7

Companies now organize certain types of work in three shifts according to the world's three main time zones: the Americas, East Asia/Australia and Europe. The 'working day' has no meaning in a global village where electronic communication can happen at any time of day or night.

Size matters less

Small companies can now offer services that, in the past, only giants could provide. What's more, the cost of starting new businesses is declining, and so more small companies will spring up. Many companies will become networks of independent specialists, more employees will therefore work in smaller units or alone. Individuals with valuable ideas can attract global venture capital. Perhaps one of the most telling features of the e-business is that increasing numbers of people can describe themselves without irony as one-person global businesses.

Customer service is changing

Enquiries and orders handled over the telephone today can be managed over the internet as a matter of course, at a considerably lower cost. In the US, it costs $1 to process a typical bank transaction in the conventional way; on the internet, the cost is just one cent.

Short-term focus becomes even shorter

Institutional investors and brokers' analysts have become very demanding of public companies. In the United States in particular, they relentlessly demand an improvement in results every quarter. Fail to deliver against this expectation and top managers are out, regardless of their past track record. Against this backdrop, companies have become reluctant to make long-term investments for fear of damaging their short-term results.

The internet levels the playing field

Companies which believe that flashy internet start-ups cannot threaten their core activities built up over years of careful planning, research, branding and marketing are wrong. The internet is helping to put small agile newcomers on a par with large corporations and are able to compete head on with them for new business.

People as the ultimate scarce resource

The key challenge for companies will be to hire and retain good people, extracting value from them, rather than allowing them to keep all the value they create for themselves. A company will constantly need to convince its best employees that working for it enhances each individual's value.

Summary

In this chapter, I have argued that the tendrils of the new e-business economy stretch wide and deep. The new information technologies that have brought dot.com businesses into being are simultaneously restructuring global markets and whole industry sectors, challenging conventional economic thinking, redefining how business is done, and impacting to varying degrees on every worker in the global market place.

Businesses are having to change – and change radically – in order to compete effectively in the web-based era: but the good news is that technological advances are opening as many windows of opportunity as they are threatening to close obsolete and outmoded ones.

Successful organizations will be those who come fully to terms with the dynamics of a borderless 24/7 market place.

ONE
E-business – the strategic dimension

In periods of transition such as the one we have been going through, it often appears as if there are new rules of competition. But as market forces play out, as they are now, the old rules regain their currency. The creation of true economic value once again becomes the final arbiter of business success.

MICHAEL PORTER, WRITING IN *HARVARD BUSINESS REVIEW*, MARCH 2001

Many have argued that the introduction of the internet into business practices renders the old rules of strategy and competitive advantage obsolete. According to Harvard Business School professor Michael Porter, the opposite is true: 'The only way [for companies to be more profitable than the average performer] is by achieving a sustainable competitive edge – by operating at a lower cost, by commanding a premium price, or by doing both.'

The internet tends to weaken industry profitability without providing proprietary operational advantages, it is therefore more important than ever for companies to distinguish themselves through strategy. The winners will be those that view the internet as a complement to, not a cannibal of, traditional ways of competing.

Many of the early internet pioneers, both the newly minted dot.coms and those well-established companies seeking an online presence, have competed in ways that violate nearly every principle in the strategy rule-book. As Porter puts it: 'Rather than focus on profits, they have chased customers indiscriminately through discounting, channel incentives, and advertising. Rather than concentrate on delivering value that earns an attractive price from customers, they have pursued indirect revenues such as advertising and click-through fees. Rather than make trade-offs they have rushed to offer every conceivable product or service'.

The good news is that it did not have to be this way – these were bad strategic choices but they were not the only options available. And these choices had little to do with the inherent business potential of the internet.

In fact, when it comes to reinforcing a distinctive strategy, Porter maintains that the internet provides a better technological platform than any previous generation of IT.

For most existing industries and established companies, the internet rarely cancels out important sources of competitive advantage; if anything, it is more likely to increase the value of those sources. But over time, says Porter, the internet itself will be neutralized as a source of advantage as all companies embrace its technology.

At which point, we may well see a return to the good old days when competitive advantages will once again explicitly derive from traditional strengths such as unique products, proprietary content and distinctive physical activities. Internet technology may be able to fortify those advantages, but it is unlikely to supplant them.

The message, then, is clear. Gaining competitive advantage in the post-internet business world does not require a radically new approach to business; and it certainly does not require the abandonment of classic economic principles that can still offer strategic value in a market place that depends on cutting-edge information technology

No, gaining competitive advantage in the early years of the 21st century is still reliant on applying proven principles of effective strategy.

Sources of strategic advantage rest where they always have – in cost competitiveness, product differentiation, ease of entering and exiting markets, and so on. The significance of the internet is in how it can impact on these traditional battlegrounds. Here are some examples:

The internet offers huge scope for cost-cutting

General Electric now does more business on its own private online market place than all the public B2B exchanges put together. Siemens hopes to cut its annual costs in the medium term by 3-5%. And there is room for more. One estimate quoted recently in *The Economist* puts the cost of e-procurement per order placed for routine office purchases at only 10% of physical procurement costs. Low-cost airlines like Ryanair have slashed their costs by using the internet to dispense with the need for tickets and to cut out travel agents. To date, only a minority of companies have got to grips with the cost-saving potential of the net. A 2001 survey by the National Association of Manufacturers found that only around 30% of American manufacturers were using the internet to sell or procure products or services.

The hare, the tortoise and the internet

Another myth, disputed by Michael Porter et al., is that the internet offers huge 'first-mover' advantages. However, companies that took to the internet relatively late and with some caution don't necessarily seem to have suffered: if anything, they seem to have gained from being able to avoid the mistakes and the huge spending of the pioneers. The fate of many internet retailers has shown that established companies can catch up relatively easily. The contrast between Britain's biggest supermarket chain, Tesco, selling its e-buying system to America's Safeway and the collapse of Webvan, the most ambitious and best-capitalized online grocery chain, is instructive. There is also a strong suggestion that the internet could well be lowering, not raising barriers to entry.

Internet only companies carry less organizational baggage

The big boys aren't having it all their own way. The arrival of new, internet-based firms that are more agile and innovative than the giants is shaking up whole industries and business sectors. Without question, the internet is helping to put some small agile newcomers on a par with large corporations and letting them compete head on with them for new business. Just as Microsoft came from virtually nowhere to usurp the market of mighty IBM, so a few years later Netscape appeared overnight and threatened to undermine the market (and the size) of Microsoft. Who will be next? And where will they come from?

He who pays the piper...

Another consequence of the growth of the internet as a business medium, says Robert Baldock in his book *The Last Days of the Giants*?, has been a shift in power from the seller to the buyer. According to Baldock, 'the convergence of computing, communications and content in the shape of personal computers (PCs) hooked up over a network to the internet has triggered a revolution in the way business is conducted. Users of these technologies have 24 hour access to almost everything, everywhere'.

The rise and fall of the middleman

Part of the paradox of the internet is that intermediaries are blessed under one business model and cursed under another.

On the positive side, internet-based search agents make it possible for these users to track down the cheapest products in seconds, and new internet-based intermediaries (the so-called 'Infomediaries') have created a new form of commerce whereby the buyer sets the price, not the seller.

On the other hand, according to the 'cursed' theory, information technology puts producers directly in contact with their customers, collapsing the distribution chain, wiping out all those who have made their living by taking orders or breaking big lots into smaller lots. A spooky technical term has been coined for this process: disintermediation. 'Middleman functions between consumers and producers are being eliminated,' the futurist Don Tapscott wrote in the influential best-seller *The Digital Economy*. Patrick McGovern, chairman of International Data Group, the world's largest high tech publisher, is even more dour. 'The intermediary is doomed,' he wrote in *Forbes ASAP*. 'Technology strips him of effectiveness.'

Internet-based alliances

The internet and digital media open up new ways to create wealth. Companies like Schwab, eBay, Cisco, MP3 and Linux have transformed the rules of competition in their industries by making revolutionary offerings to their customers. They did not achieve this alone: combining with like-minded partners with complementary skills was the key. In their book Digital Capital, Tapscott, Ticcoll and Lowy call these internet-based partnerships or alliances 'business webs', or 'b-webs' for short. A b-web, according to the authors, is 'a distinct system of suppliers, distributors, commerce services providers, infrastructure providers and customers that use the internet for their primary business communications and transactions.' Although alliance-based, a b-web typically has an identifiable lead partner which formally orchestrates their strategies and processes.

The rise of the internet, the ever increasing speed of change and the complicated networks within which organizations now conduct business have exposed the limitations of strategic models based on the single business unit using linear and static assumptions. As a result, the unit of strategic analysis has moved from the single company or business unit to the 'extended enterprise', the network of suppliers, customers and alliances, which together define an organization's ability to create core competencies and strategic advantage. Competence is now seen most often as a function of the collective knowledge available to the whole system – the enhanced network of suppliers, manufacturers, partners, investors and customers.

One thing is clear. The impact of information technology on the world as we know it has already been significant and can only increase over the coming years.

But let's keep things in perspective – the e-business supplements the traditional economy; it does not supplant it. As Kevin Kelly, one time editor of the highly influential *Wired* magazine, has put it, 'the old economies will continue to operate profitably within the deep cortex of the e-business'.

The fact is that around the world there are just as many cars and ships being constructed as ever, just as many roads being built, just as much coal being produced, as much steel being made.

It is a mistake to talk of a post-industrial era, because in reality those goods and services that were produced in the industrial era are still being produced today. The difference is where they are now being produced. Although in the UK Indian restaurants may employ more people than the steel, coal mining and ship building industries combined, 'traditional' industries are all thriving elsewhere in the world.

The simple conclusion – strategy has an e-dimension

One thing seems certain: the reach of the internet is bringing more intensified competition just about everywhere. Companies like Valeo and Cemex illustrate well the effect of being able to extend a company's competitive reach globally thanks to the internet, spreading their costs over a widening market. Does all this mean that business will, after all, be the main beneficiary of both the internet and new technology more broadly? Maybe not. For although there seems to be plenty of scope for cost-cutting and even for productivity improvements, neither may end up feeding through into greater profits. Rather, greater competition, more transparency and lower barriers to entry suggest that the biggest beneficiaries may ultimately be consumers.

Technological doors have opened wide to a new global, electronic economy. But e-business is not built simply on fast distribution of information. There is also a central premise of continuous change which by its nature requires constant improvement and innovation, and these are derived from the minds and imaginations of people. To compete, we have to innovate faster than the next person – who is trying to do the same thing. And of course, the next person could be anywhere, in just about any country in the world.

TWO
E-business – the global dimension

Globalization is made possible by the active exchange and utilization of information.

DANIEL BURRUS, BURRUS RESEARCH ASSOCIATES INC.

Globalization, which can be defined as the integration of economic activity across national or regional boundaries, has had a mixed press in recent times. On the one hand resented and denounced, most forcibly through demonstrations at Genoa in July 2001 and Seattle in November 1999; on the other hand seen by some as a desirable opening up of fresh market places and, in any case, inevitable.

John Micklethwait and Adrian Wooldridge, who both work at *The Economist*, have explored the globalization phenomenon in their book *A Future Perfecti*, which they wrote with two explicit aims:

> 'The first is to apply some order to the maelstrom of facts, images and opinions concerning globalization. In part that means unraveling some of the myths that have been built up about it: that is ushering in an age of global products; that it has killed inflation and changed the rules of economics; that big, local companies will crush their smaller rivals; and that geography means nothing in an age of rootless capitalism. Rather than treat globalization as one great co-ordinated movement – or, even more misleadingly, as an accomplished fact – we will argue that it should be seen as a series of waves, rather like the Industrial Revolution... The second aim... is to make [an] intellectual case for globalization. For many economists – perhaps too many – that project is too easy to waste time over. Of course globalization makes sense:

> it leads to a more efficient use of resources; any student who understands the basic tenets of comparative advantage understands that.
>
> Though hard to dispute this argument seems inadequate for two reasons. First, it fails to confront the harsh questions concerning those people who lose on account of globalization, not just economically but socially and culturally. And, second, it undersells globalization: the process has not to do only with economic efficiency; it has to do with freedom. Globalization offers the chance to fulfil (or at least come considerably closer to fulfilling) the goals that classical liberal philosophers first identified several centuries ago and that still underpin Western democracy.'

Embracing these two aims, Micklethwait and Wooldridge take us on a global journey, ranging from the shanty towns of Sao Paulo to a London townhouse that has revolutionized the telecommunications industry, and from the borders of Russia to the sex industry in the San Fernando valley. In the course of this journey, they explore some of the central issues at the heart of the globalization debate. Can the nation-state survive the politics of interdependence? Should businesses go global and what are the secrets of business success in a global age? Are we creating a winner-take-all society? What should and what can be done about the losers from globalization?

It's clear then that globalization, both as a process of international integration and growing interconnection, is not just a business phenomenon, but also a political, social, and cultural one.

And it's a continuing phenomenon. Eric Hobsbawn expresses this well in his book *The New Century*:

> 'We are certainly a single global economy compared with 30 years ago, but we can say with equal certainty that we'll be even more globalized in 2050, and very much more in 2100. Globalization is not the product of a single action, like switching on a light or starting a car engine. It is a historical process that has undoubtedly speeded up enormously in the last ten years, but it is a perma-

nent, constant transformation. It is not at all clear, therefore, at what stage we can say it has reached its final destination and can be considered complete. This is principally because it essentially involves expanding across a globe that is by its very nature varied geographically, climatically, and historically. This reality imposes certain limitations on the unification of the entire planet. However, we are all agreed that globalization, and especially the globalized economy, has made such spectacular progress that today you couldn't talk of an international division of labor as we did before the '70s.'

So what are the implications of globalization for anybody involved in formulating or implementing strategy in a business? Here are a selection of factors that company strategists may need to bear in mind, depending on the nature and scope of their enterprise:

1. Your biggest competitor is less likely to be down the road and more likely to be based on another continent. Although sometimes, paradoxically, if you remove barriers, the advantages that come from being based in a particular place, like Silicon Valley or Hollywood, can matter more rather than less.

2. Size isn't everything. The big faceless corporations won't necessarily rule. If anything, globalization tends to help small companies by bringing the world to their door.

3. There will be an increasing number of global products but even these global brands will often need to adapt to national markets, and even to micro-markets within the national market. Coca-Cola has to change its formula just to keep different parts of Japan happy.

4. The strong economies retain some advantage. As Micklethwait and Wooldridge have put it, 'The doctrine of competitive advantage is wonderful if you have advantages with which to be competitive'.

5. That said, the removal of barriers does make it a little easier for people in poor countries to compete with those in rich

ones. Combine this with the spread of management ideas, the flow of capital, and – to recap the e-dimension – technological revolution that is making computer power ever cheaper, and it does make it easier for poor people to compete on something approaching equal terms.

6. Globalization opens people's minds to an unprecedented range of ideas and influences. Free trade allows ordinary people to buy from whichever company they choose – the inevitable consequence is that customers are going to be presented with ever more choice and, as a consequence, will get ever more picky. Being adequate at what you do will become an increasingly unsustainable strategy.
7. Importers have a strong financial interest in a globalized economy. But so do exporters dependent on imported parts and machinery. Industrialists with interests in ports, shipping, international warehousing and other aspects of international trade and commerce may also see globalization as beneficial to their sectors of the economy.
8. Mergers and alliances on an ever grander scale are a feature of the global economy. The big are getting bigger. However, despite their market share and continuing growth, the top 200 companies continue to employ only a fraction of the world's workers. In 1999, they employed less than 1% of the world's workforce, compared with their 27% share of world economic activity. And while corporate profits grew three and a half-fold between 1983 and 1999, the number of people employed by these same companies only increased by 14.4%.
9. There are increasing levels of regulation for companies to contend with. The refusal by the European Union in July 2001 to countenance the merger of two American companies, General Electric and Honeywell, caused outrage in the United States. All the evidence is that the world's antitrust and financial regulators face a more difficult job than before, but their authority is not obviously less than it was.

Before we get too carried away, let's bear in mind that there are those who remain sceptical about the extent of the impact of globalization. Francis Fukuyama, for one, has expressed his doubts: 'I think that in many respects, globalization is still superficial. Although there is a great deal of talk about it currently, the underlying truth is that the global economy is still limited. It seems to me that the real layer of globalization is restricted to the capital markets. In most other areas, institutions remain intensely local…Trade, for example, is still predominantly regional.'

Perhaps the heart of Fukuyama's message is that the globalization story is not yet fully played out. Already, though, we can draw some overall conclusions. And a key conclusion for the business strategist is that globalization does not equate to homogenization. As consumers seek more choice, so companies that find themselves stretched to deliver what customers want will fall prey to others that can accommodate their needs.

So perhaps the over-riding impact of globalization on business strategy is that it intensifies the need for companies to strive for excellence. Jack Welch, as ever, states it succinctly: 'The winning companies in the global competition will be those companies that can put together the best of research, engineering, design, manufacturing, distribution –wherever they can get it, anywhere in the world – and the best of each of these will not come from one country or from one continent'.

Let's stick together: the importance of clusters

In his 1990 book *The Competitive Advantage of Nations*, Michael Porter defined clusters as 'geographic concentrations of interconnected companies, specialized suppliers, service providers, firms in related industries, and associated institutions in particular fields that compete but also cooperate'. Probably the two best known clusters, and certainly the mostly widely cited, are Silicon Valley and Hollywood.

In a global economy, there is, on the face of it, every opportunity for companies competing in related industries to be based just about anywhere that has reasonable access to the relevant market place. In a 1999 interview, Michael Porter seized on this apparent paradox:

'In a global economy where it's easy to move goods and information around the world, these things become givens available to any enterprise. As a result, they are no longer a source of competitive advantage. The decisive, enduring advantages, therefore, become unique local centers of innovation for the likes of mutual funds, venture capital, and biotechnology in Greater Boston or aircraft equipment and design, boat and shipbuilding, and metal fabrication in Seattle. The list of clusters goes on and on, both in this country and abroad. With the proximity that clusters provide, companies can do things together without formal ownership or legal relationships. And this kind of flexibility opens up more possibilities for change and dynamism, which are crucial ingredients in a modern economy, where prosperity depends on innovation.'

So, it seems, even in an age of globalization, local economic circumstances still matter. Although clusters are most common in the advanced economies, they are also one of the essential steps for countries aiming to move in that direction.

And how are clusters nurtured in emerging nations? In Costa Rica, for instance, with a long history of investing in education, a cluster in information technology began to develop a number of years ago. Porter tells the story: 'Eventually [that] convinced Intel to build a plant there. Related actions followed, including supplier upgrading programs and modernization of the airport. Building a true cluster in Costa Rica will take decades to complete, but I'm confident that it will be sustainable because the country offers some unique qualities that are a source of competitive advantage – among them, the highest computer usage in Latin America. Without these, all the intervention in the world won't help'.

For their book, John Micklethwait and Adrian Wooldridge spent a long time examining companies that formed part of the Silicon Valley cluster with the goal of pinning down the cultural attributes that have proved vital to the Valley's success. Here are what they termed 'the ten habits of highly successful clusters':

1. **A firm belief in meritocracy**: The Valley endlessly renews itself by bringing in new brains.
2. **An extremely high tolerance for failure**: Hardly surprising then that internet companies gravitated towards Silicon Valley.
3. **Tolerance of treachery**: Neither secrets nor staff are kept for long, but this is accepted as the inevitable consequence of running talent-intensive businesses.
4. **Collaboration**: Companies and individuals regularly form short- term alliances.
5. **A penchant for risk**: There's an attitude that one winner will pay for scores of failures.
6. **Reinvestment back into the cluster**: Unusually, money made in the Valley tends to be ploughed back into the Valley, thus helping to guarantee the continuing health of the cluster.
7. **Enthusiasm for change**: Companies fear that to get stuck in a rut is to risk ending up dead.
8. **Obsession with the product**: In part this is driven by the knowledge that winning products tend to get enormous market shares.
9. **Generous opportunity**: Success is admired and aspired to rather than begrudged.
10. **Strong inclination towards sharing wealth**: When Valley firms are sold, the founders more often than not share a sizeable amount of the proceeds with company workers.

THREE
E-business – the organizational dimension

To note that information technology is having an impact on organizations is on a par with saying that Madonna seems to notch up the occasional column inch in the newspapers. Despite those gainsayers who have noted the demise of innumerable dot.coms with a certain *schadenfreude*, the fact is that the impact of the internet and allied technologies has already been significant and can only increase over the coming years.

When it comes to assessing that impact, however, we hit a small problem. There's a well known aphorism that if you want to find out about water, then don't go asking a fish. Just as water quickly becomes unremarkable when you spend all your time swimming in it, so we humans have a remarkable capacity for accommodating technological change with barely a second glance.

And yet all the major technologies have significant, if subtle, impact on the way we work and live. Take the light bulb. Before the invention of the electric light by Thomas Edison, people used to sleep an average of ten hours a night. These days, we sleep on average for just over seven hours, with a third of people getting by on less than six hours. More recently, the mobile phone has gone from being the stuff of futuristic science programmes to commonplace in a handful of years.

In terms of extent and speed of impact, though, the internet has outpaced all of the great disruptive technologies of the 20th century – electricity, the telephone, the motor car, and so on. Amid everything else it is doing, the internet is re-inventing the nature of work.

There are plenty of people writing about the impact of technology at a high level. There is no doubt that technology has enabled the creation of a global market place. Books and articles abound on 'the death of distance', 'the conquest of location', the irrelevance of size, the subjugation of time, and so on.

The internet and organizations

In terms of our day-to-day experience, here are just some of the ways in which the internet is changing the fabric of our working lives:

Most internet businesses are built on greenfield sites

There are very few Chief Executives of more traditional, bricks-and-mortar companies who would admit to being totally happy with the structure, shape and size of their organizations.

Also, it seems that most CEOs are pretty unenamoured of the people that work for them and alongside them. A survey carried out a few years ago by the Institute of Directors and Development Dimensions International asked senior directors what percentage of their employees they would re-hire if they could change all their employees overnight. Half said they would re-hire between 0% and 40%. Only 7%, moreover, expressed confidence in the leadership capabilities of their peers within their organizations.

Internet start-ups do not face these problems, at least not in the early days. The organization is consciously designed and the people involved are handpicked. They do not, in short, suffer from what a CEO chum of mine calls 'inherited incompetence'.

Hierarchy

A traditional organization is structured around two key concepts – the breakdown and management of goals and tasks through the use of hierarchy and stable employee relationships over prolonged periods of time. In internet organizations, structures are more flexible and dynamic. Hierarchy has not vanished but it has been augmented by distributed lattices of interconnections.

In an interview on The Motley Fool Radio Show in April 2000, CEO Tim Koogle, described the set-up at Yahoo!: "It's not hierarchical. We do have a structure in the company because you need a structure to have some order on things, but it's a pretty flat organization".

For well-established organizations, Shoshana Zuboff of the Harvard Business School believes that a rigid hierarchy gets in the way of making best use of technology. She writes: 'The successful reinvention of the firm consistent with the demands of an information economy will continue to be tragically limited as long as the principal features of modern work are preserved. Unlocking the promise of an information economy now depends on dismantling the very same managerial hierarchy that once brought greatness'.

Decision making

In an e-business, as with more traditional businesses, the leadership team typically make all the big strategic decisions about what the company is going to do. The difference is that decision-making in e-businesses is often a more collaborative process. At Yahoo! for example, Tim Koogle has described how working in adjoining cubicles affects the leadership team's approach to decision-making: 'During a normal day, you'll find us hollering back and forth across the wall, bouncing around inside the cubes, grabbing each and going off into a little conference room'.

Another facet of decision making in internet start-ups is that companies grow too fast to be managed closely from the centre. Decisions, once taken centrally, are rapidly devolved to those working in the business to determine the method and manner of implementation.

Internal communication

This is not a problem for e-businesses in the early days when the organization consists of a small group of highly motivated people who spend a lot of time in each other's company, and who therefore automatically keep themselves and each other in the picture. However, business growth needs to be fuelled by new blood. By definition these are people who were not part of the original set-up and therefore processes and systems need to be introduced to ensure that everybody is kept informed – it no longer happens naturally.

For internet businesses, the speed of growth means that the need for more formalized communication systems can kick in very quickly. The ill-fated boo.com, for example, went from 12 or so people to over 400 in less than a year.

The working day now lasts 24 hours

Information technology has the capacity not only to change where knowledge and power reside in the organization; it also changes time. The 'working day' has less meaning in a global village where communication via electronic mail, voice mail, and facsimile transmissions can be sent or received at any time of day or night. Paradoxically, as the working day has expanded, so time has contracted. Companies compete on speed, using effective co-ordination of resources to reduce the time needed to develop new products, deliver orders or react to customer requests.

Growth has been de-coupled from employment

Particularly during the 1980s, it became more and more apparent that the real bottom line of technology was that it made jobs go away. It didn't happen all at once. But, starting in the manufacturing industries and then moving into white-collar work, every day more work was either being automated or relocated to other parts of the world with lower labour costs.

Not enough good people to go around

For most e-businesses, the factor that limits or enables rapid growth is their capacity to recruit and retain good people. Finding the right people to sustain rapid growth is problematic for any business at any stage of its lifecycle. For an unproven e-business start-up, particularly now that the internet economy has lost its luster, it can be virtually impossible. Significantly, most of the consultancy fees paid by e-business start-ups to date have gone to specialist recruitment companies.

The workplace becomes transparent

Shoshana Zuboff argues in an article for *Scientific American* that information technologies transform work at every organizational level by potentially giving all employees a comprehensive, or near comprehensive, view of the entire business. These technologies surrender knowledge to anyone with the requisite skills. This contrasts with earlier generations of technological advance where the primary impact of new machines was to decrease the complexity of tasks.

Technology also facilitates the open sharing of know-how within a company. By and large, e-businesses have a better track record at knowledge management. Many traditional companies retain a 'knowledge is power' mentality, and even those that consciously set out to create a knowledge sharing environment can fall foul of knowledge-hoarding by suspicious business units or individuals fearful of becoming dispensable.

The rise of the virtual organization

Virtual organizations are formed by a cluster of interested parties to achieve a specific aim – perhaps to bring a specific product or idea to market – and then disappear when the aim has been achieved. The concept is not just a useful tactic for corporate downsizing, it also carries ideological weight. Manuel Castells argues that 'it is not accidental that the metaphor – virtual – is cybernetic, for the information highway facilitates a loose corporate web connected by modem rather than physical affinity or long-term relationship. The worker brings to the market place only his human capital. The virtual corporation pays only for the value the worker can add. If the worker gets weary of the insecurity, the solution is obvious. He should become an entrepreneur himself. We are all Bill Gates – or at least we should be'.

Working from home

It is now perfectly possible for a worker to be based at home using e-mail and other technology to communicate with colleagues and the outside world generally. In fact, it's estimated that around one in five of us spend at least a part of our working year based at home. In reality, this isn't what most people want from work. It is significant that even the high-tech pioneers tend to cluster in hotspots like Silicon Valley to enable them to talk with and learn from like-minded others.

The impact of technology – a final thought

The introduction to this chapter discussed the remarkable capacity we have to absorb new technologies like the mobile phone. And it's probably true – we can cope with singular new technologies which augment a previous technology by adding a new feature, e.g. from fixed base phones to mobiles. But the internet's impact on working life is different. It doesn't just augment, it transforms our experience of work. It transforms where we work, how we work, when we work – it even transforms whether we work. The job for life has disappeared, never to return. Working life has never felt so insecure for so many.

So perhaps the real issue is not the capacity of the technology, it's our capacity to cope. Shoshana Zuboff certainly believes that the technological tail is wagging the human dog. In just 15 words from her book *In the Age of the Smart Machine* – a book all the more remarkable for being written back in the 1980s – Zuboff sums up the challenge we now face.

'So far,' she writes, 'patterns of morality, sociality, and feeling are evolving much more slowly than technology'.

The rise of the cyber cottage industry

In recent years, Tom Peters, co-author of *In Search of Excellence* and probably the world's best known management guru, has been looking at how changes at a corporate, national and global level impact on the nature of work for us as individuals. It is a topical theme that takes a variety of guises – knowledge workers making a living out of Charles Leadbeater's 'thin air'; McKinsey warning its clients that the biggest challenge for companies is 'the war for talent'; Tom Peters' 'brand called you'; Harriet Rubin's 'soloists'; business magazines like *Fast Company* devoted to Me Inc. or me.com and full of advice on 'why it pays to quit,' how you should be hotdesking with colleagues, telecommuting from home, and generally reconsidering your whole future.

Charles Handy paints this picture of the 21st century world of work: 'It's obviously going to be a different kind of world… It will be a world of fleas and elephants, of large conglomerates and small individual entities, of large political and economic blocs and small countries. The smart thing is to be the flea on the back of the elephant. Think of Ireland and the EU, or consultants and the BBC. A flea can be global as easily as one of the elephants but can more easily be swept away. Elephants are a guarantee of continuity but fleas provide the innovation. There will also be ad hoc organizations, temporary alliances of fleas and elephants to deliver a particular project.'

The internet gives added impetus to anybody considering the 'flea' life, either totally on their own or with a cluster of like minds. In *The Death of Distance*, Frances Cairncross describes how, by using technology creatively, small companies can now offer services that, in the past, only giants could provide. What's more, the cost of starting new businesses is declining, and so more small companies will spring up. Many companies will become networks of independent specialists; more employees will therefore work in smaller units or alone.

Individuals with valuable ideas can attract global venture capital. Perhaps one of the most telling features of the e-business is that increasing numbers of people can describe themselves without irony as one-person global companies.

FOUR
The e-business gurus

The task of selecting the key gurus in the field of e-business is a little daunting. All too often, people who are hailed initially as ground-breaking thinkers or business players have, within a couple of years, been fully absorbed into the e-business bloodstream, their once stunning insights reduced to the status of the blindingly obvious.

In selecting gurus for inclusion in this book, every effort has been made to pick out those individuals who still have something of practical value to offer the reader. They are a mix of academics, writers, consultants and industry players.

That said, there will inevitably be one or two gurus featured in this book whose impact will be short-lived and whose place in the book will prove to be undeserved. It is equally inevitable that there will be new players and thinkers appearing in the weeks, months and years ahead who would merit inclusion.

These issues will be addressed by the publication in due course of a second edition. In the meantime, here are potted introductions to a selection of people whose common feature is that they all challenge our thinking about and/or inform our understanding of the world of e-business.

Each of these short sections will describe why the person featured qualifies as an e-business guru, and most sections will have the following features:

- **Claim to fame**: A snappy encapsulation of the significance of the person featured.
- **E-bite**: A short, pithy quote of something the guru has said or written that illustrates their perspective.

- **Reality check**: A clear-eyed assessment of the guru's contribution to the e-business field.
- **Connectivity**: Where applicable, a pointer to the reader to check out how a guru's contribution dovetails or contrasts with the other gurus featured in this chapter of the book.
- **Sources and further reading**: Key written works by or about the guru.

The people featured in this section are as follows:

1 Tim Berners-Lee
2 Jeff Bezos
3 Frances Cairncross
4 Manuel Castells
5 Jim Clark
6 Michael Dell
7 Larry Downes & Chunka Mui
8 Peter Drucker
9 Esther Dyson
10 Philip Evans & Thomas Wurster
11 Carla Fiorina
12 Bill Gates
13 William Gibson
14 Andy Grove
15 Michael Hammer
16 Jonathan Ive
17 Steve Jobs
18 Kevin Kelly
19 Ray Kurzweil
20 Charles Leadbeater
21 James Martin
22 Gerry McGovern
23 Regis McKenna
24 Robert Metcalfe
25 Paul Mockapetris
26 Geoffrey A. Moore
27 Gordon Moore
28 John Naisbitt
29 Nicholas Negroponte
30 Larry Page & Sergey Brin
31 Jeff Papows
32 Don Peppers & Martha Rogers
33 Michael Porter
34 David S. Pottruck & Harry Pearce
35 Thomas Stewart
36 Alvin Toffler
37 Linus Torvalds
38 Meg Whitman
39 Niklas Zennström
40 Shoshana Zuboff

1 Tim Berners-Lee

Claim to fame

Inventor of the world wide web in 1989.

The internet started life as ARPANET (Advanced Research Project Agency Network), a computer network that the US Department of Defense set up in 1969. The original aim of ARPANET was to enable computer scientists and engineers working on military contracts all over America to share expensive computers and other resources. For security reasons, the network had to be able to continue working even if some cables connecting these computers were destroyed. The solution was to develop a computer network that had no fixed centre and no fixed routes. Each computer connects to a small number of neighbours, which in turn have a few different neighbours.

In 1983, ARPANET split into MILNET, for military use, and ARPANET for academic and scientific research.

What finally pulled the net from its academic and military roots and set it on its way to becoming the global phenomenon we now know as the world wide web, was invented in 1989 by Tim Berners-Lee, a British researcher at CERN's European Laboratory for Particle Physics in Switzerland. Berners-Lee was also responsible for establishing a standard for addressing (URLs), linking language and transferring multi-media documents on the Web (HTML and HTTP).

In his book *Weaving the Web*, Berners-Lee describes his role in bringing about the world wide web and in making the web the basis of today's communications revolution.

What comes over clearly is his idealism. An astute man, he certainly appreciated the commercial potential of his invention, whose intellectual property rights could probably have made him richer than Bill Gates. And yet he turned his back on vast riches, opting instead to work for the common good.

That said, his altruism is tempered by realism. He fully recognizes, for example, that the internet has potential downsides if mishandled. Evan Schwartz, in his book *Digital Darwinism*, records a conversation in which Berners-Lee outlines one of his concerns:

> '"What if telecom companies start handing out PCs for free to sign you up for 'Internet service and show you ads?" Actually, this is something that has already happened and it greatly disturbs Berners-Lee. He sees a danger in bundling everything together this way. "I was brought up on *The Times* of London," he says, "which people buy for its editorial independence. But nowadays, the search button on the browser no longer provides an objective search but a commercial one. Hardware comes with software that sells rather than informs."'
>
> The web is most powerful not as a mass medium, he has suggested, but rather a means for organizing communities, niche markets, and teams within companies. 'I'm less happy with the incentive for reaching a global audience,' Berners-Lee has written. 'The good news is that intranets are bringing the technology back into corporations to be used as a group tool.'
>
> In the future, he says, the web will be more fun, will blend better into everyday life, and will be something that doesn't even require computers as we've come to know them. "Your kids will be rummaging through boxes of breakfast cereal," he once mused, "and they'll say: 'What is this?' And they'll pull it out and unroll it, and it will be magnetic, and they'll put it on the refrigerator, and start browsing the web with it."

> **E-bite**
>
> *'We certainly need a structure that will avoid those two catastrophes:the global uniform McDonald's monoculture, and the isolated Heaven's Gate cults that understand only themselves. By each of us spreading our attention evenly between groups of different size, from personal to global, we help avoid these extremes.'*
>
> TIM BERNERS-LEE, WEAVING THE WEB

Reality check

As well as his misgivings about the possible impact of commercial factors on the development of the Net, there are other aspects of Berners-Lee's vision for the internet that has yet to be fully realized. He hoped, for example, that the internet would become as much a publication's medium as a public information source. He believed that the net provided an opportunity for individuals to participate actively in building collective knowledge. The surfer would be no mere viewer of information but rather an engaged contributor to change. The internet, he hoped, would become a medium that can codify the sum total of human knowledge and understanding.

Potted biography

A graduate of Oxford University, Tim Berners-Lee is currently the director of the World Wide Web Consortium (W3C), Senior Researcher at MIT's CSAIL and Professor of Computer Science at Southampton University. Prior to working at CERN, he was a founding director of Image Computer Systems, a consultant in hardware and software design, real-time communication graphics and text processing, and a principal engineer with Plessey Telecommunications.

Connectivity

For a fuller appreciation of some of the technical intricacies involved in creating the internet as we know it, see Paul Mockapetris.

Sources and further reading

Tim Berners-Lee, *Weaving the Web: The Past, Present and Future of the World Wide Web by its Inventor,* Orion Business Books, 1999

2 Jeff Bezos

Claim to fame

Founder of online giant Amazon.

Today, Amazon – the brainchild of Jeff Bezos – is one of the few internet brands that is recognized just about anywhere in the world. From its very early days, it has had a clear vision, namely to be 'the world's most customer-centric company. The place where people come to find and discover anything they might want to buy on-line'.

Underpinning that vision are the company's six core values:

- Customer obsession
- Ownership
- Bias for action
- Frugality
- High hiring bar
- Innovation

Amazon is a classic example of an organization whose values have a physical embodiment in the shape of its founder. Jeff Bezos' actions and behaviour shape and frame the company's culture.

For example, in the early days of the company, Bezos took every opportunity to spend only the minimum necessary. On one famous occasion, he went to Home Depot and bought three wooden doors for $60, from which he fashioned three desks. The story entered Amazon folklore and is an excellent illustration of how a core value – in this case, frugality – can be reinforced by a symbolic (and, as it happens, highly practical) act.

Bezos also regularly implores his people to be customer obsessed. "Wake up every morning terrified," he once told a meeting of company employers, "not of the competition but of our customers".

Although it was Bezos' realization in 1994 that internet usage was growing at a significant rate that set the entire online retailing phenomenon in motion, it is the personal stamp that he puts on the business that more than anything has enabled Amazon to become the world's best known and most highly regarded online book retailer.

E-bite

'There are two kinds of companies, those that work to try to charge more and those that work to charge less. We will be the second.'

JEFF BEZOS

Reality check

Of course, Amazon has long since evolved from an online bookseller into a mass retailer, but many of the company's core practices were developed in its early days. The use of behavioural targeting, for example, to suggest products its customers might like based on their past purchases. Bezos was also among the first to spot that the transparent pricing and product information the internet was able to provide would allow people to shop just about anywhere. The trick, therefore, was to make it easier for them, so these days Amazon's website now operates as a shop front for many other companies as well.

Potted biography

Jeffrey Preston Bezos was born in 1964 in Albuquerque, New Mexico. In 1986, he graduated from Princeton in Computer Science and Electrical Engineering. After a few years working for a high tech start up company called Fitel, he joined finance company, D.E. Shaw and Co., where he rose to become their youngest ever Vice President.

After much planning and research, Bezos left the security of his Wall Street job to pursue his hunch that the internet offered some exciting opportunities for online retail.

Amazon.com came into existence on July 16, 1995 and became a publicly traded company in 1997.

Connectivity

For more on the other great online retail success story eBay, see Meg Whitman.

Sources and further reading

Bernard Ryan, *Jeff Bezos: Business Executive and Founder of Amazon.Com,* Facts on File Inc, 2005

Rebecca Saunders, *Business the Amazon.com Way: Secrets of the World's Most Astonishing Web Business,* Capstone, 1999

3 Frances Cairncross

Claim to fame

Senior Editor at *The Economist* and lucid reporter from the front-line of the IT revolution.

Readers of *The Economist* will be familiar with the work of Frances Cairncross who has been a senior editor there since 1984. Between 1994 and 1997, when she was in charge of the magazine's media and communications, she wrote two surveys on the global telecommunications industry which formed the basis for the first edition of her book *The Death of Distance* in 1997.

Written in the same approachable style that makes a high level of technical knowledge unnecessary, *The Death of Distance* does nothing less than map out how converging communications technology are reshaping the economic, commercial and political landscape.

Unlike many writers on information technology and the communications revolution, she does not simply describe what she sees. Rather, she explores the practical ramifications of these advances for the way in which we work and live. She has tackled, inter alia, the connection between IT developments and the changing nature of organizations, communities, government authority, popular culture, and languages. Hers is a staggering achievement in synthesis helped, no doubt, by access to the formidable resources of *The Economist*.

In *The Death of Distance*, Cairncross sets outs a number of developments in information and communication technology that she believes will impact on industry and society in the not-so-distant future. Here are some examples:

- **The death of distance**: Distance will no longer determine the cost of communicating electronically. Companies will organize certain types of work in three shifts according to the world's three main time zones.
- **The fate of location**: Companies will locate any screen-based activity wherever they can find the best bargain of skills and productivity.
- **The irrelevance of size**: Small companies will offer services that, in the past, only giants could provide. Individuals with valuable ideas will attract global venture capital.
- **A deluge of information**: Because people's capacity to absorb new information will not increase, they will need filters to sift, process and edit it.
- **Communities of practice**: Common interests, experiences, and pursuits rather than proximity will bind communities together.
- **The loose-knit corporation**: Many companies will become networks of independent specialists; more employees will therefore work in smaller units or alone.
- **More minnows, more giants**: On one hand, the cost of starting new businesses will decline, and companies will more easily buy in services so that more small companies will spring up. On the other hand, communication amplifies the strength of brands and the power of networks.
- **The proliferation of ideas**: New ideas and information will travel faster to the remotest corners of the world. Third world countries will have access to knowledge that the industrial world has long enjoyed.
- **The shift from government policing to self-policing**: As content sweeps across national borders, it will be harder to

enforce laws banning child pornography, libel and other criminal or subversive material and those protecting copyright and other intellectual property.

- **Redistribution of wages**: Low-wage competition will reduce the earning power of many people in rich countries employed in routine screen-based tasks, but the premium for certain skills will grow.
- **Rebalance of political power**: Rulers and representatives will become more sensitive to lobbying and public opinion polls, especially in established democracies.
- **Global peace**: As countries become even more economically interdependent, people will communicate more freely and learn more about the ideas and aspirations of human beings in other parts of the globe. The effect will be to increase understanding, foster tolerance, and ultimately promote worldwide peace.

E-bite

'The death of distance as a determinant of the cost of communications will probably be the single most important economic force shaping society in the first half of the next century. It will alter, in ways that are only dimly imaginable, decisions about where people live and work; concepts of national borders; patterns of international trade.'

FRANCES CAIRNCROSS, IN A 1995 SURVEY OF THE TELECOMMUNICATIONS INDUSTRY PUBLISHED IN *THE ECONOMIST*

Potted biography

Frances Cairncross is a senior editor at *The Economist*, where she has worked since 1984. She is an honorary fellow of St Anne's College, Oxford, and a visiting fellow of Nuffield College, Oxford. She has an honorary doctorate from Glasgow University.

Reality check

In the ten years or so since the book was published, some of the specific, technology-based phenomena that she predicted have indeed come to pass. Some developing countries, for example, now routinely perform on-line services – monitoring security screens, running help-lines and call centres, writing software, and so forth. Much of the social and political change she anticipated, however, has yet to show through to any meaningful level. And global peace seems as far away now as it did in 1995.

Yet in truth, the value of *The Death of Distance* does not rest in whether Cairncross has a good accuracy rate with her predictions. Like any good history of the future, the value lies more in the extent to which Cairncross manages to challenge assumptions and provoke the reader's thinking.

Connectivity

To learn the views of some other key industry commentators, see Esther Dyson and Regis McKenna.

Sources and further reading

Frances Cairncross, *The Death of Distance*, Orion Publishing, 1997

The Economist website can be found at www.economist.com

4 Manuel Castells

Claim to fame

European academic with a commanding grasp of the social and economic impact of the new technology.

Kevin Kelly, former editor of *Wired* magazine, has described Manuel Castells as 'a sociologist with a European's bent for the large-scale sweep of history'. His magnum opus, and the main reason he features as an e-guru, is his sprawling, literate, visionary and densely argued trilogy *The Information Age*

In an age when all too many e-business texts stretch a meagre handful of ideas beyond breaking point, *The Information Age* is like trading up from the bargain red in the local supermarket to a classy Bordeaux. His trilogy is rich, complex and improving with age.

In *The Rise of the Network Society*, published in 1996, he offers a catalogue of evidence for the arrival of a new global, networked-based culture. For Castells, the Network Society is characterized by, amongst other things:

- The globalization of strategically decisive economic activities.
- The networking form of organization.
- The flexibility and instability of work.
- The individualization of labour.

The book goes on to examine the processes of globalization that have marginalized whole countries and peoples by leaving them excluded from informational networks.

In the second book of the trilogy, *The Power of Identity*, published in 1997, Castells gives his account of two conflicting trends shaping the world: globalization and identity. The book explores how the development of an information technology world is impacted by proactive movements, such as feminism and environmentalism, and reactive movements like religion, nationalism and ethnicity.The final volume of a trilogy, *End of Millennium*, published in 1998 looks at processes of global social change induced by interaction between networks and identity.

For virtually all of the three volumes, Castells declines to engage in futurology. However, he concludes the final volume of the trilogy by setting out 'some trends that may configure society in the early 21st century'. His key predictions are that we may well see:

- The information technology revolution accelerating its transformative potential, and as a result technology will achieve its potential to unleash productivity.
- The full flowering of the genetic revolution.
- The continuing and relentless expansion of the global economy.
- The survival of nation states, but not necessarily their sovereignty
- The 'exclusion of the excluders by the excluded', i.e. those who do not have the capability to participate in the information economy will become more tribal in outlook.

Reality check

How then to sum up this trilogy? First of all, it has to be said that Castells is not an easy or quick read: he is a large canvas thinker, the three books run to almost 1500 pages, and the text and style often fit what you might expect from a European academic! That said, and even if he goes occasionally into over-exhaustive detail, Castells writes with intelligence and obvious insight. For a systematic interpretation of the global information economy world at the turn of the millennium, Castells has no equal.

E-bite

'The 21st century will not be a dark age. Neither will it deliver to most people the bounties promised by the most extraordinary technological revolution in history. Rather, it may well be characterized by informed bewilderment.'

MANUEL CASTELLS, *THE INFORMATION AGE*

Potted biography

Born is Spain in 1942, Manuel Castells is recognized as one of the world's leading social thinkers and researchers.He is Professor of Sociology, and of Planning at the University of California, Berkeley, where he was appointed in 1979. Prior to this, Castells spent 12 years teaching at the University of Paris. He has published over 20 books.

Connectivity

Castell's research-based view of the internet and its workings is arguably matched by only Peter Drucker for depth of insight and gravitas.

Sources and further reading

Manuel Castells, *The Information Age: Economy, Society and Culture,* Blackwell Publishers Ltd., Oxford

- Volume I: *The Rise of the Network Society,* 1996
- Volume II: *The Power of Identity,* 1997
- Volume III: *End of Millennium,* 1998

Castells has also contributed a 22-page essay entitled *'Information Technology and Global Capitalism'* to a collection edited by Will Hutton and Anthony Giddens called *On the Edge: Living with Global Capitalism,* Jonathan Cape, London, 2000.

5 Jim Clark

Claim to fame

Serial entrepreneur and billionaire who founded Netscape and Silicon Graphics.

When Jim Clark decided to take Netscape public just 18 months after forming the company in 1994, despite it having no profits and no revenue to speak of, he rewrote the laws of capitalism. He was the first new economy entrepreneur to show that a company's potential for massive growth was a more critical factor in its value than the need to show real or imminent profits.

The Netscape flotation, on August 9, 1995, remains perhaps the most famous share offering in the American stock market's history. It was a huge success with the company's stock doubling in value within less than 24 hours. It also set the scene for a series of high-profile flotations by, amongst others, eBay, priceline.com and MarketWatch.

Clark is now a billionaire on the back on his entrepreneurial exploits.

So what does Jim Clark's story tell us about the e-business? That Clark is its Citizen Kane? That the aura and mystique of a larger-than-life character like Clark plays a bigger part in selling a business idea than a convincing business plan? That Silicon Valley, the engine-room of the e-business, has a surreal sense of business logic?

The curiosity is, that of the three enterprises Clark is most closely associated with, Silicon Graphics is struggling to survive, Netscape was sold to online giant AOL, and his venture into the US healthcare market through his company Healtheon proved too ambitious and ended up in a merger with the Microsoft-backed WebMD.

E-bite

The moment of conception was, to Clark's way of thinking, the critical moment of any new enterprise. At that moment it was important not merely to hire the people bent on changing the world but to avoid hiring the people bent only on changing jobs.

"There are all sorts of guys who will show up because they can't think of anything else to do," he said. "Those are exactly the people you don't want. I have a strategy for dealing with these people. When they come by to apply for a job I tell them, 'We're all confused here. We don't know what we're going to do yet.' But when you find someone you want, I tell them, 'Here's exactly what we're going to do and it is going to be huge and you are going to get very, very rich.'"

TAKEN FROM *THE NEW NEW THING* BY MICHAEL LEWIS

Reality check

Clark's strategy for dealing with venture capitalists – sell the dream, not the business plan, and you're in – is all very well and works for him. But in terms of business lessons for the general reader, you can take it that no VC is going to treat you the way Clark is treated – unless you too are worth a few billion.

It has also been said of Clark that his undoubted nose for a good start-up opportunity is undermined by his reputation as a somewhat impatient investor with little apparent interest in building a company for the long term.

Potted biography

Jim Clark taught as an Assistant Professor at the University of California from 1974-78 and as an Associate Professor at Stanford University from 1979-1982. He founded Silicon Graphics in 1981, Netscape in the mid-90s and Healtheon a few years later. He recently launched two more start-ups, MyCFO.com, a personal finance site for the ultra-rich, and Shutterfly.com, an online photographic processing and delivery service.

Connectivity

For another insight into the heady days of Silicon Valley in the 1990s, see the story of Vermeer Technologies in Chapter 5.

Sources and further reading

Michael Lewis, *The New New Thing: How Some Man You've Never Heard Of Just Changed Your Life*, W W Norton, 1999

Joshua Quittner and Michelle Slatalla, *Speeding the Net*, Atlantic Monthly Press, 1998

Worth reading for a more detailed insight into Jim Clark in the Netscape days. Written by the technology editors from *Time* magazine and *The New York Times*, respectively.

6 Michael Dell

Claim to fame

Started up the best known direct sales company dealing in personal computers and peripherals.

If a storyline of 'precocious child becomes successful business leader' has you reaching for the corporate sick bag, then you'll need to approach Michael Dell with care. At the age of 12, he earned $2,000 buying and selling stamps, and by the time he was 18, he was selling customized personal computers.

In 1985, he dropped out of his biology course at Austin University in Texas and started the Dell Computer Corporation. Under his leadership, the company has gone on to become one of the most successful computer businesses in the world, redefining the industry with its direct-sale approach and the customer support model it pioneered. Dell was one of the very first companies to market PCs by phone and subsequently to sell online using the web.

The key, then, to the success of Michael Dell's business model is selling direct. Dell eliminates the middleman by custom-building IBM clones and selling them directly to consumers, thereby reducing overhead costs and eliminating dealer mark-ups. So Dell's customers perceive that they are getting a good deal relative to other computer sellers while at the same time Dell is making more profit per computer sale than any of its rivals.

Underpinning this model is a very disciplined approach to inventory management – Dell carries very little pre-made stock – and a set of relationships with suppliers that Dell relies on absolutely to meet its quality standards (Dell does not manufacture any components – it simply assembles them).

E-bite

'Think about the customer, not the competition. Competitors represent your industry's past, as, over the years, collective habits become ingrained. Customers are your future, representing new opportunities, ideas, and avenues for growth.'

TAKEN FROM *DIRECT FROM DELL* BY MICHAEL DELL

Reality check

Michael Dell has undoubtedly played a very significant part in building the global PC market. However, one or two critics have started to suggest that Dell's model is beginning to run out of stream, and so a real question mark lingers over whether Dell will be as significant to the future of the e-business as he has been in helping to bring it about.

Potted biography

Texan billionaire Michael Dell is Chairman and Chief Executive Officer of Dell Computer Corporation. He is a member of the Board of Directors of the United States Chamber of Commerce and the Computerworld/Smithsonian Awards.

Connectivity

Michael Dell's success can be partly attributed to the effectiveness of his internet-based business model. For more on the two other biggest online success stories, Amazon and eBay, see Jeff Bezos and Meg Whitman.

Sources and further reading

Michael Dell, *Direct from Dell*, HarperBusiness, 1999

Rebecca Saunders, *Business the Dell Way*, Capstone, 1999

7 Larry Downes & Chunka Mui

Claim to fame

Invented concept of the killer app to describe the disruptive capability of technology.

Here's a question: What do longbows, light bulbs, Henry Ford's Model Ts and atomic bombs have in common?

The answer: They are all what writers and consultants Larry Downes and Chunka Mui call killer apps (short for applications), in other words inventions whose impact has extended far beyond the activities for which their creators made them.

In their book *Unleashing the Killer App: Digital Strategies for Market Dominance*, Downes and Mui define a killer app as 'a new good or service that establishes an entirely new category and, by being first, dominates it, returning several hundred percent on the initial investment... Killer apps are the Holy Grail of technology investors, the stuff of which their silicon dreams are made'.

Most companies view killer apps with mixed feelings. On the one hand, they have the potential to earn enormous sums of money for companies. On the other, killers apps are, in the words of Downes and Mui, 'like the Hindu god Shiva. They are both regenerative and destructive.' They can create enormous opportunities but they also displace older, unrelated older offerings, and so destroy and re-create industries far from their immediate use. As a result, they can throw into disarray the complex relationships between business partners, competitors, customers, and regulators of markets.

Today's killer apps spring mainly from the digital realm, i.e. from the transformation of information into digital form, where it can be manipulated by computers and transmitted by networks. Over the past ten years, the world wide web, personal computers, e-mail and – more recently – mobile phone technology have reshaped both our working and social worlds in ways that we are still grappling to come to terms with.

Implicit in their concept of digital strategy is a view that the classical approach to strategy – top-down, analytical, based on a thorough understanding of the market place, executing carefully developed plans over a period of time – has little place in a killer app universe. Digital strategy has two guiding principles: the first is that the best way to predict the future is to invent it, and the second suggests that the future is unknowable beyond – at most – a 12-18 month time frame. That strategy therefore needs to become a real-time, dynamic, intuitive process.

Reality check

In *Unleashing the Killer App*, Downes and Mui have provided budding digital strategists with a useful set of lenses for understanding the new e-conomy, as well as some convincing advice about how to prosper in the digital world. But be warned – below the surface there is a more disquieting message. No matter what your company does or its size or market position, there's probably a killer app lurking out there somewhere that will redefine your business world, and probably sooner than you might care to imagine!

E-bite

'Technology change initially affects technology, but once critical mass is reached, the disruption takes place in other, unrelated systems. Television redefines the relationships of family and community; cloning challenges basic understandings and definitions of character and personhood. Electronic commerce has caught national and local governments completely off guard, and while they scamper to figure out how to apply whomever's law, the technology continues to evolve into forms less and less analogous to enterprises with which they are familiar. These are the types of changes that historian Thomas Kuhn, in a much more limited context, first referred to in 1962 as paradigm shifts, discoveries so fundamental that they knock out the basic pillars of universally held beliefs, requiring that brand new structures be built to explain them. In the case of digital technology, the new structure is called cyberspace.'

TAKEN FROM *UNLEASHING THE KILLER APP* BY DOWNES AND MUI

Potted biographies

Born in 1959, Larry Downes is a consultant with over 20 years' experience of working with global businesses. He also teaches law and technology at Northwestern University.

Chunka Mui is Executive Editor of the business magazine *Context* and a Partner with Diamond Technology Partners. He is also Director of the Diamond Exchange, a forum for exploring issues in digital strategy.

Connectivity

See Kevin Kelly for another big picture account of the significance of the internet economy.

Sources and further reading

Larry Downes and Chunka Mui, *Unleashing the Killer App: Digital Strategies for Market Dominance,* Harvard Business School Press, 1998

Downes and Mui have developed a companion website, which allows budding digital strategists to communicate and share thinking. If you're interested, check out www.killer-apps.com.

8 Peter Drucker

Claim to fame

The first of the e-business gurus. Originated the concept of knowledge working.

Peter Drucker has spent 50 years proving himself to be most prescient business-trend spotter of our time. Back in the 1950s, he was describing how computer technology would transform business. Although many of us might think that the concept of knowledge working dates back ten or 20 years at most, in fact Drucker coined the term as far back as 1954.

In his book *The Age of Discontinuity*, published in 1969, he described with great clarity and perception the forces of change that were to transform the economic landscape and the nature of society over the following 20 to 30 years. In particular, he discerned four major areas of discontinuity underlying the then social and cultural reality:

- The rapid emergence of new technologies resulting in major new industries.
- The emergence of the global economy.
- A new socio-political reality of pluralistic institutions that would pose drastic political, philosophical, and spiritual challenges to government and society.
- The emergence of knowledge as the new capital and the central resource of the economy, with significant implications for mass education, work, leisure, and leadership.

It is this last area in which Drucker has been a commanding presence. He foresaw that the rise of knowledge work would inevitably cause significant change in the workplace. He wrote in *The Age of Discontinuity* that 'knowledge work itself knows no hierarchy, for there are no "higher" and "lower" knowledges. Knowledge is either relevant to a given task or irrelevant to it. The task decides, not the name, the age, or the budget of the discipline, or the rank of the individual plying it... Knowledge, therefore, has to be organized as a team in which the task decides who is in charge, when, for what, and for how long.'

Drucker also recognized that the 'knowledge worker' would be a new breed of employee, and would therefore need a more subtle form of management: 'Though the knowledge worker is not a labourer,' he wrote, 'and certainly not proletarian, he is not a subordinate in the sense that he can be told what to do; he is paid, on the contrary, for applying his knowledge, exercising his judgement, and taking responsible leadership'.

The knowledge worker, Drucker predicted, would be a very different creature to the loyal, subservient 'organization man': 'The knowledge worker sees himself just as another professional, no different from the lawyer, the teacher, the preacher, the doctor or the government servant of yesterday. He has the same education. He has more income, he has probably greater opportunities as well. He may well realize that he depends on the organization for access to income and opportunity, and that without the investment the organization has made... there would be no job for him, but he also realizes, and rightly so, that the organization equally depends on him'.

Drucker's foresight extended well beyond the workplace. He recognized that the transition from the industrial age to the information age would profoundly change society, business and government. Knowledge would confer tremendous power on those who possessed it.

Reality check

Drucker stands up as possibly the most prescient management guru of all time. Back in the 1950s and 1960s, Drucker uncovered a future world of work that nobody else detected.

E-bite

Peter Drucker chronicles the rise of the knowledge worker 1954-1969:

'In the United States ... the class of employees that has been growing most rapidly in numbers and proportion is that of skilled and trained people.'

THE PRACTICE OF MANAGEMENT (1954)

'Productive work in today's society and economy is work that applies vision, knowledge and concepts — work that is based on the mind rather than the hand.'

LANDMARKS OF TOMORROW (1959)

'Even the small business today consists increasingly of people who apply knowledge rather than manual skill and muscle to work.'

MANAGING FOR RESULTS (1964)

'Every knowledge worker in modern organization is an 'executive' if, by virtue of his position or knowledge, he is responsible for a contribution that materially affects the capacity of the organization to perform and to obtain results.'

THE EFFECTIVE EXECUTIVE (1966)

> *'Finally, these new industries differ from the traditional 'modern' industry in that they will employ predominantly knowledge workers rather than manual workers.'*
>
> THE AGE OF DISCONTINUITY (1969)

Connectivity

Peter Drucker has been around long enough to have valid links to just about every other guru in this book! As just one example, have a look at Thomas Stewart for a complementary view of the significance of knowledge management.

Potted biography

Born in 1909 in Vienna, Peter Ferdinand Drucker was educated in Austria and then England, where he took his doctorate in public and international law. He began his career as a newspaper reporter in Frankfurt. He subsequently worked for various banks and companies in London before moving to America in 1937. He took a succession of academic appointments before moving to California in 1971 to become Clark Professor of Social Science at Claremont Graduate School. He has received honorary degrees from universities in the U.S., Belgium, Great Britain, Japan, Spain and Switzerland. Now in his 90s, he still writes occasionally for *The Wall Street Journal* and the *Harvard Business Review*.

Sources and further reading

Peter Drucker, *The Age of Discontinuity*, Heinemann, 1969

Peter Drucker, *Management Challenges* for the 21st Century, HarperCollins, 1999

Peter Drucker, *Post-Capitalistic Society*, HarperCollins, 1993

An early picture of e-business which has held up extremely well over the intervening years.

9 Esther Dyson

Claim to fame

E-business insider with the ability to explain complex ideas to the non-technical reader.

Esther Dyson has attracted a lot of labels over the years – entrepreneur, high-tech industry analyst, first lady of the internet, government adviser, and queen of the digerati amongst others.

She came to fame as the president and owner of Edventures Holdings, and as the driving force behind *Release 1.0*, a respected monthly newsletter for the high-tech industry. In 1997, she published a book – *Release 2.0* – for which she 're-purposed' and augmented material that featured in her newsletter.

Dyson writes with an insider's knowledge, but in a way that most readers will find insightful, accessible and pertinent. Although she is occasionally berated by e-business insiders for being a mere populariser of ideas rather than a true original thinker in her own right, she merits 'guru' status for her ability to convey complex information to the non-technical reader.

Reality check

It's unfair to suggest that Esther Dyson simply transmits information without adding value. Take the following section from *Release 2.1*, a revised version of *Release 2.0* published in 1998, for example, in which she puts her individual stamp on with the following 'design rules for living':

- **Use your own judgment**: Many newcomers to the internet are tempted to defer to others, believing them to be better informed and with a deeper understanding of net issues. The net provides an opportunity for you to take soundings but trust your own views.
- **Disclose yourself**: Let others know what you stand for.
- **Trust but verify**: Use the net to check the credentials of strangers and organizations.
- **Contribute to the communities you love or build your own**: There's nothing more satisfying than creating a community in collaboration with others. If you can't find a community to accomplish something you think should happen, design and build your own.
- **Assert your own rights and respect those of others**: Acknowledge the net's capability for two-way interaction.
- **Don't get into silly fights**: It's easier to walk away from fights on the Net than it is in real life. Bypass the offending person or entity rather than get provoked.
- **Ask questions**: The Net is a great place to ask questions because you are more likely to be able to find someone who knows the answer.
- **Be a producer**: The real promise of the net is that it lets you be a producer without all the overhead that used to accompany the production process.
- **Always make new mistakes**: The challenge is not to avoid mistakes, but to learn from them.
- **Now design your own rules.**

E-bite

'The value of e-commerce is not in the 'e' but in the commerce.'

ESTHER DYSON, WRITING IN *MANAGEMENT TODAY*, JUNE 2000

Potted biography

Esther Dyson is President and Owner of Edventure Holdings, but is perhaps best know for publishing *Release 1.0*, a monthly newsletter on developments in information technology. She has written articles for the *New York Times, Harvard Business Review, Wired* and the *Washington Post*. Sister of George Dyson, author of *Darwin among the Machines*, she lives in New York City.

Connectivity

Esther Dyson is one of the more lucid and insightful industry commentators/consultants. For a UK view of the industry, have a look at Charles Leadbeater.

Sources and further reading

Esther Dyson, *Release 2.1, a Design for Living in the Digital Age*, Broadway Books, 1998

The Edventure Holdings website is located at www.edventure.com

10 Philip Evans & Thomas Wurster

Claim to fame

Early explorers of how new communication technologies enabled more sophisticated customization of information.

Those of us in the business of communicating information to others have until now faced a strategic choice, which Philip Evans and Thomas Wurster, co-authors of *Blown to Bits*, characterize as richness versus reach.

Do we seek to produce highly customized – hence rich – information about a product or service, which necessarily limits the number of potential customers that can be reached with that information? Or, do we go for reach, i.e. seeking to get our content to the greatest possible number of people and accepting that this enables only a limited degree of customization?

This simple yet apparently absolute trade-off has long stood at the centre of the information business. But according to Evans and Wurster, two consultants from the Boston Consulting Group, this dilemma is fast disappearing because advanced digital technologies mean that the transmission of information no longer requires either a physical form or a physical carrier.

This, in effect, kills off the richness/reach trade-off and renders many traditional business structures and the strategies that drive them obsolete.

This is not just a matter of concern for those working in explicit 'information' businesses. Evans and Wurster argue that in every industry information is the 'glue' that holds value chains, supply chains, consumer franchises and organizations together across the entire economy.

They go on to explain how leaders can assess the vulnerability of their own businesses and respond. They also describe how a new form of disintermediation, driven by the new economics of information, threatens not just to re-segment markets, but to destroy the intermediary business model entirely.

E-bite

'As the trade-off between richness and reach blows up, economic relationships, in all their manifestations, will change radically.'

PHILIP EVANS AND THOMAS WURSTER

Reality check

Although many of the ideas explored by Evans and Wurster in *Blown to Bits* are not totally new, they do a good job of synthesizing the available information about how to create larger market share in an information age. And in their 'richness or reach' concept, they came up with a neat way of conveying an informational dilemma that the internet has helped to push towards extinction.

Potted biographies

Philip Evans is a Senior Vice President of The Boston Consulting Group in Boston. Thomas S. Wurster is a Senior Vice President of The Boston Consulting Group in Los Angeles. Evans and Wurster are co-leaders of The Boston Consulting Group's Media and Convergence Practice.

Sources and further reading

Philip Evans & Thomas Wurster, *Blown to Bits: How the New Economics of Information Transforms Strategy*, Harvard Business School Press, 2000

Philip Evans & Thomas Wurster, Getting real about virtual commerce, *Harvard Business Review*, November–December 1999

Philip Evans & Thomas Wurster, Strategy and the new economics of information, *Harvard Business Review*, September – October 1999

11 Carly Fiorina

Claim to fame

Six times voted the most powerful woman in business, but brought down by an under-achieving merger.

In February 2005, the board of directors of Hewlett-Packard announced that Carleton S. Fiorina had stepped down as Chairman and Chief Executive Officer, with immediate effect.

"Carly Fiorina came to HP to revitalize and reinvigorate the company. She had a strategic vision and put in place a plan that has given HP the capabilities to compete and win. We thank Carly for her significant leadership over the past six years as we look forward to accelerating execution of the company's strategy," commented Patricia Dunn, HP's Chairman, on behalf of the board.

Fiorina joined HP as CEO in July 1999 at a time when the technology industry was performing well and with a mandate to transform the company. In 2002, she guided and cajoled the company through one of the most controversial mergers ever, when HP combined with Compaq, against a backdrop of vocal opposition from Walter Hewlett, a son of one of HP's iconic founders, and despite a nail biting 49% of HP's shareholders voting against the move.

Compaq was a Texan company, culturally a world apart from HP's Silicon Valley forged DNA. Both companies were struggling to cope with ferocious levels of competition in the computer industry. Fiorina's goal was to mould the two into one huge yet leaner operation, with the aim of making HP's computer business as profitable as its printer business.

Things didn't quite go to plan. Most industry observers felt that the merger caused HP to lose its focus and to find itself being squeezed by its two major rivals, Dell and IBM. Whereas Dell had a clear reputation for good quality PCs at a good price, and IBM for gluing together astonishingly complex subsystems, HP's USP seemed less apparent.

Fiorina, to be fair, disagreed with this analysis. For over two years, she maintained that HP was far from being stuck in the middle. Dell, she said represented "low tech and low cost", while IBM, with its legions of well paid technology consultants, offered "high tech and high cost". Only HP, she claimed, could offer "high tech and low cost" and therefore "the best customer experience".

However, her confidence that positive synergies would come through given time was seemingly offset by a diminishing level of confidence amongst HP board members that Fiorina could deliver. Tellingly, Patricia Dunn claimed that Fiorina's departure was "not a change related to strategy" but rather "a change...to accelerate the strategy".

E-bite

'I think the company's success will be my legacy. The company's failure will be my failure, with all the predictable consequences of that.'

CARLY FIORINA

Reality check

Financially, HP performed pretty well during Fiorina's spell as leader, with both profits and revenues jumping substantially, a chunk of which can be attributed to the Compaq merger. That said, HP continues to face pressure in several key markets. PC sales continue to suffer in competition with Dell; meanwhile IBM and EMC are attracting significant chunks of the corporate computing market. The bright star continues to be HP's printing-and-imaging division, which still generates more than 75% of the company's profits. Ironically, this was the division least toyed with by Fiorina.

Connectivity

For another view of managing a high-profile company, see Jeff Papows, who managed the Lotus Development Corporation.

Potted biography

After business school, Carly Fiorina's first job was AT&T. She spent 16 years at Ma Bell and another three years at Lucent Technologies, eventually becoming president of Lucent's global service provider business before snaring the top job at Hewlett-Packard which she joined in 1999.

Fiorina holds positions on the executive board of the New York Stock Exchange, MIT, and the World Economic Foundation. She is a fellow of the London Business School. She was listed by *Fortune* magazine as the most powerful woman in business for six years in a row until 2004, when the honour went to eBay CEO Meg Whitman.

Sources and further reading

Peter Burrows, *Backfire: Carly Fiorina's High-stakes Battle for the Soul of Hewlett-Packard*, John Wiley, 2003

'Exit Carl', The Economist, February 10th 2005

12 Bill Gates

Claim to fame

Founder and head of the Microsoft Corporation. Oh, and just about the wealthiest person in the world.

In 1974, at the age of 19, Bill Gates set up the Microsoft Corp., a computer software firm, with Paul Allen. After spending the early years converting existing software packages, their big break came in 1980 when they secured an agreement with IBM to produce the operating system for use with the personal computer being developed at the time. The system they developed, MS-DOS (Microsoft Disk Operating System), and subsequent programs (including the Windows operating systems) have made Microsoft incomparably the world's largest producer of software for PCs.

Allen left the company in 1983 for health reasons but remained a member of Microsoft's board of directors until 2000. Extremely wealthy in his own right, he has proved a shrewd investor in hi-tech companies like Starwave, America Online and Ticketmaster.

Meanwhile, Gates developed and built Microsoft through the 1980s and 1990s, along the way gaining a reputation for fierce competitiveness and aggressive business savvy, and building a huge stockpile of personal wealth.

Today, Microsoft is undoubtedly the most significant and influential software company in the world, although not the most innovative. In fact, for some time, Microsoft's strategy has been less about being at the absolute forefront of software development, and more about waiting to see what its rivals come up with and then piling into the market place relying on the company's vast resources to win market share.

For this reason, Microsoft has its critics, who complain that the company rarely offers the best software solutions – most experts reckon that Linux is a better operating system, for example, but simply relies on its market dominance to swamp its rivals' efforts. Against this backdrop, Microsoft is regularly involved in anti-trust disputes, although to date its dominant position has not been significantly affected.

Reality check

Whether you love or loathe Bill Gates, whether you admire or despair of Microsoft, there's no doubt that Gates and his company are significant global players. Antitrust hearings aside, what Gates says will happen in the world of technology has more than a fair chance of coming to pass. Barring a spectacular fall from grace, the chances are that, for some years to come, when Bill speaks, the world will still need to pay attention.

E-bite

'Microsoft has been innovating for the information worker for more than two decades – and in many ways we've only just begun to scratch the surface of how software can help people realize their full potential.'

TAKEN FROM *THE NEW WORLD OF WORK* BY BILL GATES, ONE IN AN OCCASIONAL SERIES OF E-MAILS TO MICROSOFT CUSTOMERS, DATED 19TH MAY 2005.

Potted biography

Born in 1955, Bill Gates developed an interest in programming in his teen years. He went to Harvard, and during his first year there developed a version of the programming language BASIC for the first microcomputer, the MITS Altair. He left Harvard in 1975 to co-found Microsoft with his childhood friend Paul Allen. Under Gates' leadership, Microsoft has become the world's most success software company.

Connectivity

For an insight into somebody who has been described as Microsoft's nemesis, have a look at Linus Torvalds, the man who created the Linux operating system.

Sources and further reading

William H. Gates, *Business @ the Speed of Thought,* Warner Books, 1999

William H. Gates, *The Road Ahead,* Warner Books, 1995

To prove that Bill's crystal ball is just as foggy as everybody else's, *The Road Ahead* devoted only 20 pages to the topic of the internet.

13 William Gibson

Claim to fame

Novelist who coined the term 'cyberspace'.

From H. G. Wells and Jules Verne onwards, there has been a long-standing literary tradition of the sooth-saying novelist, in other words somebody who illuminates our understanding of the future through the medium of fiction. For those of us with an interest in e-business, perhaps the most significant author to emerge in recent times has been William Gibson.

Gibson has produced a body of work over the last 20 years or so which continually informs and provokes as it entertains. His influence on many of the key thinkers in the e-business field is unmatched by any other fiction writer – just flick through an index or bibliography or one or two of the key e-business texts and the chances are that Gibson will be mentioned.

Perhaps his most notable contribution to e-business thinking can be found in his 1984 classic *Neuromancer*, in which he introduces the reader to the concept of 'cyberspace'. Here's the relevant passage from the book:

> 'Cyberspace. A consensual hallucination experienced daily by billions of legitimate operators, in every nation, by children being taught mathematical concepts … A graphic representation of data abstracted from the banks of every computer in the human system. Unthinkable complexity. Lines of light arranged in the non-space of the mind, clusters and constellations of data. Like city lights receding …'

Neuromancer was recognized almost immediately as a dark, powerful and astonishingly prescient science fiction novel, and it went on to win three notable science fiction prizes: the Hugo Award, the Nebula Award and the Philip K. Dick Memorial award.

Kevin Kelly, in his book *Out of Control* offers this brilliant encapsulation of cyberspace as originally envisioned by Gibson:

> 'Cyberspace encompasses the realm of large electronic networks which are invisibly spreading 'underneath' the industrial world in a kind of virtual sprawl. In the near future, according to Gibson's science-fiction, cyberspace explorers would 'jack in' to a borderless maze of electronic data banks and videogame like worlds. A cyberspace scout sits in a dark room and then plugs a modem directly into his brain. Thus jacked in, he cerebrally navigates the invisible world of abstracted information, as if he were racing through an infinite library ... Cyberspace is the mall of network culture. It's that territory where the counterintuitive logic of distributed networks meets the odd behavior of human society. And it is expanding rapidly. Because of network economics, cyberspace is a resource that increases the more it is used.'

It is Gibson's depiction of a fully connected world and his exploration of the concept of virtual reality that earn him his place as an e-business visionary.

Reality check

Gibson writes extremely well, avoiding the over-descriptive verbosity that afflict many sci-fi writers and leaves a satisfying resonance in the mind. However, if you can't stand the thought of picking up a science fiction book, the good news is that *Neuromancer* is less required reading and more a book to shamelessly namedrop in the presence of impressionable colleagues.

E-bite

'The future is here. It's just not widely distributed yet.'

WILLIAM GIBSON

Connectivity

Gibson is the only novelist featured in this book. For the views of a non-fiction big thinker, go to Kevin Kelly, who is possibly the only other guru featured to match Gibson for breadth of imagination.

Potted biography

William Gibson lives in Vancouver, Canada. His recent books include *All Tomorrow's Parties*, published in 1999, which reintroduces characters from *Virtual Light* and *Idoru* to complete a stunningly imagined trilogy. His latest book, *Pattern Recognition*, is regarded by many as his best since *Neuromancer*.

Sources and further reading

William Gibson, *Neuromancer*, HarperCollins, 1984

14 Andy Grove

Claim to fame

Founder and former CEO of Intel who combines an insider's knowledge with a highly strategic perspective.

Once dubbed 'the best manager in the world' by *Fortune* magazine, Andy Grove is also one of the world's best-known business figures. A co-founder of Intel in 1979, he helped the company grow into what it is today – the world's largest computer chipmaker, not to mention a regular presence in lists of the most admired and most profitable companies in America.

Luckily for us, Grove has written widely about his managerial philosophy and thinking, most notably in his book *Only the Paranoid Survive,* a lesson in leadership and strategy that could benefit any manager in any industry.

Grove provides a lens through which to view the challenges posed by an ever-changing business environment, and offers a set of strategic tools to help managers recognize and successfully address those changes. For example, he takes Michael Porter's Five Forces model and adds a sixth element, the concept of 'Complementors'. These are businesses from whom customers buy complementary products, e.g. computers need software, software needs computers. He calls complementors 'fellow travellers'. In Intel's case, their most significant complementor is Microsoft, which helps explain Grove's vocal support for Bill Gates during the Antitrust hearings.

A linked concept is what he calls an '10X factor', 'When a Wal-mart moves into a small town,' he writes, 'the environment changes for every retailer in that town. An '10X' factor has arrived. When the technology for sound in movies became popular, every silent actor and actress personally experiences the '10X' factor of technological change.'

An '10X factor' brings massive change into the dynamics of an industry. Examples include the first online bank, Amazon's entry into the book market and the mobile phone.

If '10X' factors are the drivers of massive change, strategic inflection points (SIPS) are those moments in the life history of a business when such change occurs. 'During an SIP,' Grove writes, 'the way a business operates, the very structure and concept of the business, undergoes a change. But the irony is that at that point itself nothing much happens. That subtle point is like the eye of the hurricane... when it moves the wind hits you again. That is what happens in the middle of the transformation from one business model to another'.

SIPs are his 'big idea' (such that his original title for the book was *'Strategic Inflection Points'* until his publishers stepped in with the rather more marketable *Only the Paranoid Survive*). They are a vital tool in helping companies scan the horizon for seismic changes that can rewrite industry rules.

SIPs are not limited to high-tech industries like Intel, but are particularly prevalent in the e-business. And the internet may just be the biggest SIP of all. Grove believes that within five years 'all companies will be internet companies or they won't be companies at all. In other words, companies not using the internet to improve just about every facet of their business operation will be destroyed by competitors who do'.

Reality check

Although Grove is one of life's techno-determinists, it's becoming increasing difficult to quibble with his take on the business world. What is exciting and disquieting in equal measure is his view that, as far as the internet is concerned, we are still in the hurricane's eye.

> **E-bite**
>
> *'Within five years all companies will be internet companies or they won't be companies at all. In other words, companies not using the internet to improve just about every facet of their business operation will be destroyed by competitors who do.'*
>
> ANDY GROVE, *ONLY THE PARANOID SURVIVE*

Potted biography

Born in Hungary in 1936, Andy Grove emigrated to the US in 1956. After graduating with a PhD from the University of California at Berkeley, he joined the Fairchild Semiconductor Corp., before co-founding Intel in 1979. He stepped down as CEO of Intel in 1998.

Connectivity

Grove has a strategist's mind and has drawn on the work of Michael Porter as a basis for some of his thinking and ideas. Refer to Michael Porter to find out what a classical strategist like him makes of the internet.

Sources and further reading

Andrew S. Grove, *Only the Paranoid Survive: How to Exploit the Crisis Points that Challenge every Company and Career,* HarperCollins-Business, 1996

Tim Jackson, *Inside Intel,* HarperCollins, 1997
A less flattering picture of Grove and Intel by a British journalist.

Michael Porter, *Competitive Strategy,* Free Press, 1980

15 Michael Hammer

Claim to fame

The man who popularized the concept and practice of business process reengineering.

Mike Hammer, former MIT professor is widely regarded as the originator and prime driver behind the business reengineering movement. He defines business process redesign as 'the fundamental rethinking and radical redesign of business processes to achieve dramatic improvements in critical, contemporary measures of performance'.

Business process reengineering is a management mongrel. On one side, its ancestors are Japanese theories about lean, flexible, just in time production, and on the other side, American ideas about redesigning companies from the bottom up. Since this may well mean a company having to rethink its processes and quite possibly start again from scratch, it can be an awesome task. However, process reengineering should not be an aim in itself; rather it should be linked directly to the strategic objectives of the organization.

Reengineering in general and, Mike Hammer in particular, faced much hostile criticism because the tool was used to justify an unprecedented bout of corporate bloodletting in the first half of the 1990s.

These days, reengineering has a lower profile but, according to Hammer, is more widely applied than ever. Having started out in the back office of large manufacturing companies, it has now moved into front office functions like sales, marketing and product development. In recent times, many service companies have applied it to improve their performance. Reengineering has been taken on board by smaller companies, and is also being applied across and between companies in improving supply chains.

Reality check

Process redesign should not be confused with crude cost-cutting exercises (such as downsizing), although many organizations have used both approaches simultaneously, with the result that the value of process redesign has been permanently tarnished in the eyes of many managers. Business process redesign has probably generated more negative press than any other management technique of the past decade.

We must also be careful not to equate successful change solely with dramatic transformation at the organizational level. Incremental improvement is also vital to the successful implementation of strategy. Most continuous improvement is bottom up, based on knowledge and depends on the existence of a culture in which people are empowered. It is usually incremental – move a filing cabinet, redesign a form, change the sequence of doing something, adapt an existing design, and so forth.

E-bite

'The single most important thing you can do to help your company thrive in the modern era of tough customers, intense competition, and relentless change is this: help every single person in the company understand the business in the same big-picture terms that the CEO does. Everyone needs to understand the economics of the company and its industry, its strategy and cost structure, its processes, products, and competitors.

'You can do that step-by-step. Start by developing a process map of the company's business that shows how value is created and where costs are incurred. Make sure everyone knows who the customers are and what they need. Share an appreciation of industry themes and the company's strategic direction.'

MICHAEL HAMMER, QUOTED IN *FAST COMPANY*, SEPTEMBER 2001

Potted biographies

Dr Michael Hammer is generally credited with being the originator and leading exponent of the concept of business reengineering. He was named by *Business Week* magazine as one of the four pre-eminent management gurus of the 1990s.

Sources and further reading

Michael Hammer and James Champy, Reengineering the Corporation, *HarperCollins Publishers*, 1993

Information Strategy, October 1998. Features an interview with Hammer.

Daniel Pink, 'Who has the next big idea?', *Fast Company,* September 2001

16 Jonathan Ive

Claim to fame

Apple's award winning Vice-President of Industrial Design.

In June 2005, The Royal Academy of Engineering awarded its coveted Silver President's Medal Apple to Jonathan Ive. He had previously been the winner of the Design Museum's first Designer of the Year prize in 2003.

As Vice-President of Industrial Design at Apple, Ive is the man behind a whole wave of innovative, eye-catching and yet highly functional Apple products over the past few years, including the iMac, iBook, Cube, Powerbook G4, and more recently, the ubiquitous iPod – a product that propelled Apple from a niche player, whose products were more admired than bought, to a truly significant global operator.

Ive has attributed his success to what he calls Apple's 'fanatical care beyond the obvious stuff' as shown by the company's relentless experiments into new tools, materials and production processes.

But when he joined Apple back in 1992, the company was in a slump. Ives recalled those early days in an interview with The Design Museum:

> 'The company was in decline. It seemed to have lost what had once been a very clear sense of identity and purpose. Apple had started trying to compete to an agenda set by an industry that had never shared its goals. While as a designer I was certainly closer to where the decisions were being made, but I was only marginally more effective or influential than I had been as a consultant.'

How times have changed. Triggered by the return of Apple's co-founder Steve Jobs, in recent years the company has enjoyed a financial renaissance based on a return to Apple's core values based on matching style with function, and employing superb design to deliver products that are both sophisticated and rewarding to use.

While Steve Jobs has rightly been given much of the credit for this reinvigoration of the company's fortunes, many industry insiders believe that it has been the ability of Ives and his design team to deliver eye-catching yet functionally excellent products that turned the company around.

E-bite

'So many companies are competing against each other with similar agendas. Being superficially different is the goal of so many of the products we see. A preoccupation with differentiation is the concern of many corporations rather than trying to innovate and genuinely taking the time, investing the resources and caring enough to try and make something better.'

JONATHAN IVE, IN AN INTERVIEW GIVEN TO THE DESIGN MUSEUM

Reality check

At a time when so many new products are still bland and derivative, Ive is a true original. He combines a talent for innovation with a relentless focus on function. Apple products don't just look good, they also embody the highest levels of functionality, as the runaway success of the iPod has shown.

Potted biography

Born in London in 1967, Ive studied art and design at Newcastle Polytechnic before co-founding Tangerine, a design consultancy where he worked on a wide range of products from power tools to wash basins. In 1992, he accepted an offer to join Apple, one of his clients at the time, and in 1998 he was appointed Vice-President of Industrial Design at Apple.

Connectivity

For an insight into the thinking of Jonathan Ive's boss at Apple, move along one chapter to Steve Jobs.

Sources and further reading

www.designmuseum.org. An excellent and highly informative website for anybody interested in product design.

17 Steve Jobs

Claim to fame

Co-founder of Apple, innovator, and computer industry thought leader.

Steve Jobs is one of the computer industry's most iconic figures.

In 1976, he co –founded Apple with his friend Steve ('the Woz') Wozniak. Jobs and Wozniak made a highly effective team, combining Wozniak's engineering talent with Jobs's ingenuity and marketing instincts. Between them they came up with, and successfully launched, the first ready-made personal computer. Their company grew rapidly on the back of the success of their early products.

However, in 1985, he was forced to leave the company after falling out with the then CEO John Scully. During the late 80s and early 90s, Apple went into a period of decline. This sad state of affairs only changed when Jobs returned to the company in 1996, initially as an informal advisor when Apple bought NeXt, a computer company he had founded in the interim. He subsequently became Chief Executive again in 2000. Since that time, the company has flourished.

Jobs has attributed his success and Apple's revival to the fact that the company was able to re-establish its core values. In the 1970s, Apple differentiated itself by talking about being at the intersection of technology and the arts. With Jobs back at the helm, Apple once again started pursuing a direction which was clear and different from any other of the major technology companies. Jonathan Ive, Apple's VP of Industrial Design has characterized this difference as Apple's focus on ease and simplicity, and what he has called 'caring beyond the functional imperative'.

Over the past few years, he has reinvigorated the Macintosh line and overseen Apple's rival-trumping ascendancy in the digital music business through its nifty combination of the iPod player and iTunes software.

To this day, Jobs is recognized as an innovative and bold industry player, with an ongoing capacity to surprise. In June 2005, for example, he took the stage at Apple Computer's Worldwide Developers Conference to announce Apple's decision to shift the Macintosh microprocessor business to Intel after more than a decade with its longtime rival IBM.

Reality check

In the pantheon of America's greatest computer innovators, perhaps only Bill Gates can match the reputation of Steve Jobs. His extraordinary success at Apple has been reinforced in recent years with the performance of the animated film studio Pixar – maker of *Toy Story* and more recently the phenomenally successful *The Incredibles*, of which he is also the Chief Executive Officer.

Less flatteringly, Jobs, who is notoriously protective of his privacy, recently objected to an unauthorized biography by first unsuccessfully pressuring publisher John Wiley to cancel plans to release it, and then by ordering all books by the same imprint to be withdrawn from Apple shops around the world.

This response was not a one-off. In recent months, Apple has brought a round of lawsuits against individuals and websites, accusing them of unfairly disseminating secrets about upcoming Apple products.

E-bite

'A lot of companies have chosen to downsize, and maybe that was the right thing for them. We chose a different path. Our belief was that if we kept putting great products in front of customers, they would continue to open their wallets.'

STEVE JOBS

Connectivity

There is more on Apple's approach and philosophy in the section on Jonathan Ive.

Sources and further reading

Jeffrey S. Young and William L Simon, *Icon Steve Jobs: The Greatest Second Act in the History of Business*, John Wiley & Sons, 2005

The not entirely flattering book whose publication Apple tried to suppress.

18 Kevin Kelly

Claim to fame

First editor of *Wired* magazine, and author of one of **the** core e-business texts.

If the e-business needed to elect a founding father, Kevin Kelly would be on most people's list of nominations. As the first editor of *Wired* magazine in the early 1990s, Kevin Kelly quickly built a reputation as one of e-business' creators and biographers.

In his book *New Rules for the New Economy*, published in 1998, Kelly sets out to identify the underlying principles that govern how the wired world operates. His starting point is that ideas and assumptions about the nature of work and the operating patterns of organizations that stem from the Age of the Machine simply don't make sense in the revolutionary Age of the Network. Success, maintains Kelly, flows primarily from understanding networks – how they behave and the rules that govern them.

At the heart of the network revolution is communication. Kelly writes:

> 'Communication is the foundation of society, of our culture, of our humanity, of our own individual identity, and of all economic systems. This is why networks are such a big deal. Communication is so close to culture and society itself that the effects of technologizing it are beyond the scale of a mere industrial-sector cycle. Communication, and its ally computers, is a special case in economic history. Not because it happens to be the fashionable leading business sector of our day, but because its cultural, technological, and conceptual impacts reverberate at the root of our lives.'

New Rules for the New Economy takes the form of ten 'rules', each given a chapter in the book. Kelly formulated these guiding principles by asking some fundamental questions: how do our tools shape our destiny? What kind of economy is our new technology suggesting? What became clear to him was, he writes, that 'Steel ingots and rivers of oil, smokestacks and factory lines, and even tiny seeds and cud-chewing cows are all becoming enmeshed in the world of smart chips and fast band width, and sooner or later they will begin to fully obey the new rules'.

The ten rules themselves are a pithy guide to business survival in the internet age. But don't let the brevity of the book fool you – there is no evidence that Kelly has skimped on his thinking. In fact, one of his real talents is an ability to absorb and synthesize large amounts of information (his first book, *Out of Control*, came with a 300-title annotated bibliography at the back).

Reality check

A definition of genius is the ability to look at the same world as everybody else and draw different conclusions. It's an ability that Kelly clearly has in abundance. Beyond that, as his lucid writing shows, he is equally capable of reporting back what he sees.

E-bite

KEVIN KELLY'S TEN NEW RULES FOR THE NEW ECONOMY

1. **Embrace the swarm**: As power flows away from the centre, the competitive advantage belongs to those who learn how to embrace decentralized points of control.

2. **Increasing returns**: As the number of connections between people and things add up, the consequences of those connections multiply out even faster, so that initial successes aren't self-limiting, but self-feeding.

3. **Plentitude, not scarcity**: As manufacturing techniques perfect the art of making copies plentiful, value is carried by abundance, rather than scarcity, inverting traditional business propositions.

4. **Follow the free**: As resource scarcity gives way to abundance, generosity begets wealth. Following the free rehearses the inevitable fall of prices, and takes advantage of the only true scarcity: human attention.

5. **Feed the web first**: As networks entangle all commerce, a firm's primary focus shifts from maximizing the firm's value to maximizing the network's value. Unless the net survives, the firm perishes.

6. **Let go at the top**: As innovation accelerates, abandoning the highly successful in order to escape from its eventual obsolescence becomes the most difficult and yet most essential task.

7. **From places to spaces**: As physical proximity (place) is replaced by multiple interactions with anything, anytime, anywhere (space), the opportunities for intermediaries, middlemen, and mid-size niches expand greatly.

8. **No harmony, all flux**: As turbulence and instability become the norm in business, the most effective survival stance is a constant but highly selective disruption that we call innovation.

9. **Relationship tech**: As the soft trumps the hard, the most powerful technologies are those that enhance, amplify, extend, augment, distil, recall, expand, and develop soft relationships of all types.

10. **Opportunities before efficiencies**: As fortunes are made by training machines to be ever more efficient, there Is yet far greater wealth to be had by unleashing the inefficient discovery and creation of new opportunities.

TAKEN FROM *NEW RULES FOR THE NEW ECONOMY*.

Potted biography

Born in Pennsylvania and brought up in New Jersey, Kevin Kelly dropped out of college to spend eight years trekking around India, Nepal, and the Far and Middle East. On his return to the US, Kelly began to discover the on-line world, and through this he developed contacts that led to him becoming Editor of *Whole Earth Review*, before going on to became Founding Editor at *Wired*. He left the role when the magazine was sold but remains an Editor-at-Large. He is currently working on a project to list all the 30 million or so species of life on earth.

Connectivity

Nobody fizzes with provocative ideas quite like Kevin Kelly, but for a tantalising view of the technological future, have a look at Ray Kurzweil.

Sources and further reading

Kevin Kelly, *New Rules for the New Economy: 10 Ways the Network Economy is Changing Everything,* Fourth Estate, 1998

Kevin Kelly, *Out of Control: The New Biology of Machines,* Addison Wesley Inc, 1994

Kelly has a website www.kk.org/ and the full text of *Out of Control* can be found at www.kk.org/outofcontrol/index.html

Andrew Davidson, 'The Net Prophet', *The Financial Times,* 3 June 2000

Highly readable and informative article about Kelly.

19 Ray Kurzweil

> **Claim to fame**
>
> Inventor of the Law of Accelerated Returns.

Ray Kurzweil is an inventor, entrepreneur, author, and futurist. Labeled 'the restless genius' by *The Wall Street Journal* and 'the ultimate thinking machine' by Forbes, Kurzweil's ideas on the future have been endorsed and touted by his many fans, ranging from Bill Gates to Bill Clinton.

Kurzweil was the principal developer of the first omni-font optical character recognition, the first print-to-speech reading machine for the blind, the first CCD flat-bed scanner, the first text-to-speech synthesizer, the first music synthesizer capable of recreating the grand piano and other orchestral instruments, and the first commercially marketed large-vocabulary speech recognition.

But perhaps his most notable contribution in the computer technology field has been to devise the Law of Accelerating Returns. First unveiled in a 2001 essay, Kurzweil based his findings on research he carried out into measuring the computational power of machines back to the time of H. G. Wells.

Taking into account five technology paradigms, from electromechanical, through vacuum tubes to integrated circuits, Kurzweil found that the rate of technological change has been even more dramatic than that forecast by Gordon Moore's famous law (see the section on Gordon Moore for more details).

Kurzweil found that from the late Steam Age through the Electro-mechanical Age, about 30 years ago, computational power doubled every two years. But with the dawn of the Digital Age, computational power began to double yearly.

This led him to form a startling conclusion, as he reported in his 2001 essay:

> 'An analysis of the history of technology shows that technological change is exponential, contrary to the common sense 'intuitive linear' view. So we won't experience 100 years of progress in the 21st century –it will be more like 20,000 years of progress (at today's rate). The 'returns,' such as chip speed and cost-effectiveness, also increase exponentially. There's even exponential growth in the rate of exponential growth.'

Kurzweil predicts that within 20 years, we will enter what he calls the 6th paradigm of computing, when the bulk of our experiences will shift from real reality to virtual reality.

This future leads to a point where societal, scientific and economic change occurs at a speed so fast that we can't even imagine what will happen from our present perspective. According to Kurzweil, 'Within a few decades, machine intelligence will surpass human intelligence, leading to The Singularity – technological change so rapid and profound it represents a rupture in the fabric of human history. The implications include the merger of biological and nonbiological intelligence, immortal software-based humans, and ultra-high levels of intelligence that expand outward in the universe at the speed of light.'

In the longer term, he predicts that 'most of the intelligence of our civilization will ultimately be non-biological, which by the end of this century will be trillions of trillions of times more powerful than human intelligence.'

E-bite

'Now back to the future: it's widely misunderstood. Our forebears expected the future to be pretty much like their present, which had been pretty much like their past. Although exponential trends did exist a thousand years ago, they were at that very early stage where an exponential trend is so flat that it looks like no trend at all. So their lack of expectations was largely fulfilled. Today, in accordance with the common wisdom, everyone expects continuous technological progress and the social repercussions that follow. But the future will be far more surprising than most observers realize: few have truly internalized the implications of the fact that the rate of change itself is accelerating.'

RAY KURZWEIL, IN HIS ESSAY *THE LAW OF ACCELERATING RETURNS*

Reality check

Kurzweil didn't invent the Singularity, only a model for measuring our progress toward it. Singularity is generally credited to mathematician and author Vernor Vinge, who began expounding on the topic in the 1980s.

And just in case you are still sitting comfortably, beyond the Singularity could lie the Gray Goo, a concept posited by Eric Dexler of the Foresight Institute. The Gray Goo is what results when nanomachines destroy mankind. Nice to have something to look forward to!

Connectivity

Kurzweil is one of the latest writers and thinkers to speculate about our technological future. He follows a fine tradition established by the likes of futurists Alvin Toffler and John Naisbitt.

Potted biography

Ray Kurzweil is widely regarded as one of the leading inventors of our time. He was inducted in 2002 into the US National Inventor Hall of Fame. He was also awarded the 1999 National Medal of Technology, the nation's highest honor in technology by President Clinton. He has received 11 honorary doctorates, seven national and international film awards, and honors from three US presidents.

Sources and further reading

Ray Kurzweil, *The Singularity Is Near: When Humans Transcend Biology*, Viking Books, 2005

Ray Kurzweil, *The Age of Spiritual Machines: How We Will Live, Work, and Think in the New Age of Intelligent Machines*, Texere, 2001

An essay by Ray Kurzweil called *The Law of Accelerating Returns* (2001), which can be found at www.kurzweilai.net/articles

An essay by Vernor Vinge called *Technological Singularity* (1993), which can be found at www.ugcs.caltech.edu/~phoenix/vinge/vinge-sing.html

20 Charles Leadbeater

> **Claim to fame**
>
> Leading UK expert in the fields of innovation, entrepreneurship and the knowledge economy.

What do you make to earn your living? Do you make anything tangible that can be weighed, measured or touched? For most people, says Charles Leadbeater, the answer to the second question is no, with more and more of us making our living from thin air – from our ideas and our know-how. 'Knowledge,' states Leadbeater, 'is our most precious resource: we should organize society to maximize its creation and use. Our aim should be to harness the power of markets and community to the more fundamental goals of creating and spreading knowledge'.

In his book *Living on Thin Air*, Leadbeater explores the societal implications of a knowledge-driven economy, coming as it does at a time of increasing economic and job insecurity. He goes on to argue that society will need to be organized around the creation of knowledge capital and social capital, rather than simply being dominated by the power of financial capital. In *Living on Thin Air*, he writes as follows:

> 'When financial, social and knowledge capital work in harmony, through institutions designed to reconcile their competing demand, society will be strong. When these forces are at war, society will malfunction. A society devoted to financial capitalism will be unbalanced and soulless. A society devoted to social solidarity will stagnate, lacking the dynamism of radical new ideas and the discipline of the competitive market. A society devoted

solely to knowledge creation would be intelligent but poor, even if it did realize the value of its know-how to the full. When these three forces of the e-business work together, they can be hugely dynamic. Too often they seem in danger either of spinning out of control or of being trapped by a society unable to stomach the institutional reforms needed to move forward. That is where we are, trapped between the gridlock of the old and the chaos of the new.'

More recently, Leadbeater had been building his reputation in the field of innovation and entrepreneurship. When addressing the Institute of Directors Annual Convention in April 2005, he offered this piece of advice to companies: "Listen to your customers – but also listen to ideas from elsewhere, or you'll go down a dead end".

E-bite

'We are moving into an economy where the greatest value is in the recipes rather than the cakes.'

CHARLES LEADBEATER

Reality check

Leadbeater puts over his ideas in a highly informative and accessible way and argues his case well, although some readers may feel that his take on the future is a little more optimistic than the facts seem to justify.

Potted biography

Charles Leadbeater is an independent writer, a research associate for UK think-tank Demos, and an e-business consultant to leading companies. Previously, he was Industrial Editor and Tokyo Bureau

Chief at *The Financial Times* before moving on *The Independent,* where he devised *Bridget Jones's Diary* with Helen Fielding. In 1998, he helped Peter Mandelson, then Secretary of State at the Department of Trade and Industry, to develop a White Paper entitled *Building the Knowledge Driven Economy*.

Connectivity

To understand the roots of the knowledge economy, go to Peter Drucker or Thomas Stewart.

Sources and further reading

Charles Leadbeater, *Living on Thin Air,* Viking, 1999

Charles Leadbeater & Kate Oakley, *The Independents: Britain's New Cultural Entrepreneurs,* Demos, 1999

21 James Martin

> **Claim to fame**
>
> Pulitzer Prize nominated IT industry heavyweight with over 100 books to his name.

Now based in the United States, James Martin has been a significant presence in the information technology field for over three decades. A former adviser to the US government, his book *The Wired Society,* published in 1978 and nominated for a Pulitzer Prize, anticipated the arrival of cellular telephones, the world wide web, the internet and e-mails

Once ranked as the fourth most influential person in the computer industry by *Computerworld* magazine, these days, he is a major player in the IT consultancy field. He has acted as advisor to the UK government on restructuring telecommunications in Britain and changing the role of the Post Office. He has also consulted on planning, product and service strategies for the long-term future with AT&T, IBM, Honeywell, Texas Instruments and Xerox.

In 1981, he founded Headstrong, a global e-solutions provider that invents, transforms and builds digital businesses. It is the largest information engineering consulting practice in the world, with more than 30 offices worldwide.

Martin predicts that IT leadership will look a lot different in ten years, as key technology decisions will be made by business executives, and almost all maintenance and development will be outsourced or sent offshore.

E-bite

"Mankind faces huge challenges as the 21st century unfolds. It is essential that our leading thinkers commit time, energy and resources now to finding solutions to these risks and problems which could threaten the future of humanity itself."

JAMES MARTIN, IN A SPEECH MADE TO MARK HIS DONATION OF A £60M ENDOWMENT TO OXFORD UNIVERSITY (JUNE 2005)

Reality check

James Martin has impeccable e-business credentials. An industry heavyweight with a strong academic background, he is possibly read more widely within the IT industry than outside. This is a pity, because he has much that is worth sharing with the wider business community.

Potted biography

Dr Martin is a graduate of Oxford University. He holds a Masters and a doctorate degree from the university and studied at Keble College. He also holds honorary doctorates from Salford University (UK) and the Kokkaido Technical University (Japan). Dr. Martin is the Chairman of WatchIT.com, an internet-based education company. He has written over 100 book, many of which were best-sellers within the information technology industry.

Sources and further reading

James Martin, *The Wired Society: A Challenge for Tomorrow,* Prentice Hall, 1978

22 Gerry McGovern

Claim to fame

A worldwide authority on managing web content as business asset.

Gerry McGovern believes that 'community and commerce are inherently intertwined; that you can't have one without the other'. For him, what drives the internet is not technology, it's the human touch. This belief comes through strongly in a set of 'Internet Business Principles' that feature in his first book *The Caring Economy* (see the next page for more detail).

However, McGovern offers more than a touchy-feely take on the information economy. McGovern may wear his heart and values on

his sleeve, but behind the compassion is a keen, insightful and analytical intelligence that he applies in writing about a wide range of issues: the history of the internet, the nature of cyberspace, truths and myths of the information society, globalization, the strength and limitations of computers, and so on.

And, in case that list gives the impression that McGovern is a 'big themes' man, he also offers practical and implementable advice on making best use of the internet. His two most recent books are both highly rated guides to content management. He is also a highly rated conference speaker.

Here are Gerry McGovern's Ten Internet Business Principles:

1. Care. Care about your customers. Care about your staff. Care about all those connected with you. Put people first because people are where you will find your unique competitive advantage.

2. Empower all those connected with you and, where appropriate, create communities which allow you to organize around the consumer, rather than around a product or service offering.

3. Champion and focus on old people, women and children who are three key engines in The Caring Economy. Also, focus on niches and communities of interest, delivering unique products and services. In the digital age, it will pay to specialize.

4. Focus on the value you deliver, not just the costs you save. Remember, the internet is not cheap to develop for, requiring quality brands, quality people and substantial ongoing investment.

5. Let your information flow by focusing on the three properties of information. Content, structure and publication. Use information quickly and gain value from the momentum it creates.

6. Keep the communication of your information as simple as possible. Cut through the hype and don't fall into the trap of being complicated in a complex age.

7. Think digital and study the lessons that are being learnt in software development. Learn from the internet too. Remember, the best way to succeed on the internet is to imitate how the internet itself became a success and this means thinking network.

8. Learn to play, challenge the unchallengeable, think the unthinkable and encourage the heretic. Evangelise and bring other people with you. Embrace change and flow with the age.

9. Protect and build your brand and good name. Trust is not easy to establish on the internet and those who gain the consumer's trust will reap the long-term rewards.
10. Have a long-term vision of where you want to go. Don't forget the information-poor consumer. Remember that we are citizens of an increasingly connected world. For the long-term stability and prosperity of our world, we cannot continue to ignore the injustice, poverty and famine that so many of our fellow citizens must daily endure.

Taken from *The Caring Economy* by Gerry McGovern.

E-bite

'Perhaps the fundamental principle for success in the digital age in to think network.'

GERRY MCGOVERN, *THE CARING ECONOMY*

Reality check

Gerry McGovern has long recognized that knowledge, information, and content are key resources of the modern economy. How these elements are created and managed will have a significant impact on how successful we will be as individuals and/or organizations.

Connectivity

These days, McGovern's focus is very much on web content. Have a look at Philip Evans and Thomas Wurster for more insights into communicating effectively via the net.

Potted biography

Prior to setting up his own consultancy business, Gerry McGovern was Chief Executive Officer of Nua, a company that specializes in internet-driven knowledge management solutions. Born in Ireland in 1962, he gained a Bachelor of Science in Management from Trinity College, Dublin. After leaving college in 1984, he worked in business for a while before leaving to write fiction and travel. In 1994, he wrote a report for the Irish government called *Ireland: the Digital Age, the Internet*. In the following year, he and two colleagues founded Nua.

Sources and further reading

Gerry McGovern, *Content Critical*, Financial Times Prentice Hall, 2001

Gerry McGovern, *The Web Content Style Guide*, Financial Times Prentice Hall , 2001

Gerry McGovern, *The Caring Economy*, Blackrock, 1999

McGovern writes a free, weekly e-mail newsletter called *New Thinking*, which aims to contribute towards the development of a digital age business philosophy. To subscribe, go to www.gerrymcgovern.com/

23 Regis McKenna

Claim to fame

One of the first advocates of the need for companies to think 'real time'.

Most modern-day managers know that we are living in an age of ever more demanding customers. They want better quality, they want cheaper prices and, above all, they want it now.

Against this backdrop, writer and consultant Regis McKenna maintains that companies who wish to remain competitive in the market place face a stark choice – they must become a real time business or perish. This means that companies need great technology that helps to compress time, says McKenna in his book *Real Time*.

Just as critically, companies must challenge conventional wisdom about how they operate. Traditional facets of company life – hierarchy, long-term planning methodologies – need to go, to be replaced by 'real time managers' who focus on delivery and results, and who recognize that customized service is the new corporate mantra.

McKenna acknowledges that it is not easy to create a real time company, but the benefits are potentially immense. As he puts it in his book:

> 'The task of implementing a real time corporation is difficult and complex, but it is an essential investment in your competitive future. The implementation of real time systems will have the effect of changing the working relationships within your organization as well as those with your partners and customers. The application of the technology will change your corporate culture. As these

systems are adopted, new ideas for services and products, new ways of gaining customer loyalty, and new methods of team collaboration will take shape. Then information technology will indeed become a valued corporate asset.'

Reality check

When McKenna's book *Real Time* was first published, it received excellent reviews in America, and a number of well-respected CEOs – including Fred Smith of Federal Express and HP's Lew Platt – sang its praises ("McKenna's insights will excite and shock you," said Platt). Although the messages of the book seem far less radical now than when it was first published in 1977, McKenna's analysis remains just as valid, as does his emphasis on customized service and time-based competition.

> **E-bite**
>
> *'Winning organizations will be run in the expectation of relentless shifts and readjustments in the marketplace, in customers' expectations, and in the behavior of competitors. Like Lewis Carroll's Queen, they will anticipate surprises six times a day before breakfast.'*
>
> REGIS MCKENNA, *REAL TIME*

Potted biography

Regis McKenna is Chairman of The McKenna Group, based in Palo Alto, California. He regularly lectures and conducts seminars on technology marketing and competitiveness. McKenna is author of *The Regis Touch, Who's Afraid of Big Blue?* and *Relationship Marketing.*

Connectivity

For a broader view of how the internet changes the business rules, go to Frances Cairncross.

Sources and further reading

Regis McKenna, *Real Time: Preparing for the Age of the Never Satisfied Customer,* Harvard Business School Press, 1997

24 Robert Metcalfe

Claim to fame

The man whose eponymous law explains the value of networks.

Many years ago there was a story doing the rounds – doubtless apocryphal – that the person who owned the very first fax machine in the world was delighted with their buy until they realized that they had nobody to whom they could send a fax! It was only when the second fax machine in the world came online that the first machine became of value.

True or not, this story serves to illustrates what has become known over the years as Metcalfe's Law: this is an observation made by Robert Metcalfe, founder of 3Com Corporation, that networks (whether of telephones, computers, people or fax machines) dramatically increase in value with each additional node or user.

Metcalfe's Law values the utility of a network as the square of the number of its users. This can be illustrated as follows:

NUMBER OF USERS	VALUE OF NETWORK	
1	1	(i.e.1x1)
2	4	(2x2)
3	9	(3x3)
4	16	(4x4)
	and so on...	

What this boils down to for those of us involved in e-business is that users beget users. The more people who have a mobile phone, an internet connection, an e-mail address and so on, the more valuable the network becomes, and the more new users it will attract.

Reality check

Metcalfe's Law stands as an interesting counterpoint to traditional economic theory, which suggests that scarcity, rather than abundance, creates increased value. It also explains some interesting inversions of traditional business propositions. For example, why mobile phones were virtually being given away in their early days, and why downloading Google is free. To put it crudely, the lower the initial price, the more quickly critical mass is reached. Ironically, once critical mass is reached, sellers can in theory charge subsequent users more, because the growth in the network has increased the value of the application.

E-bite

'I'm an engineer and I think everyone should be engineers. I have a feeling that there are probably other life choices that are as valid as that. But other people should advocate those. I will advocate science and technology, particularly engineering, engineering being slightly different than being a scientist in the grand scheme of things. So I recommend it. It's a great life. Solving problems. Developing mastery over subjects.'

ROBERT METCALFE, IN AN INTERVIEW HE GAVE IN 2001

Potted biography

Robert Metcalfe was born in Brooklyn, New York in 1946. He went to MIT, graduating in1969 with a bachelor's degree in Electrical Engineering and Business Management. In 1970, he received a masters in Applied Mathematics from Harvard University, and he completed his PhD in Computer Science at Harvard in 1973. In 1979, Metcalfe founded the 3Com Corporation in Santa Clara, California, where he served in various roles until his departure in 1990. In March 2005, President Bush presented him with the National Medal of Technology for 2003 for his pioneering work while at the Xerox's Palo Alto Research Center (PARC) that in 1973 resulted in the invention of Ethernet. He is still active on the technology scene through his writing and public speaking.

Connectivity

For a more strategic view of the powers of networks, see Kevin Kelly. The fast growth of the internet economy has often been attributed to a combination of the impact of Metcalfe's Law and Moore's Law. See the section on Gordon Moore.

Sources and further reading

Robert Metcalfe and Peter Denning, *Beyond Calculation: Next Fifty Years of Computing*, Springer-Verlag New York Inc., 1997

25 Paul Mockapetris

Claim to fame

The man widely credited with creating the Domain Name System.

Paul Mockapetris is one of the unsung heroes of the internet. While other gurus featured in this book have made more eye-catching contributions to the e-business field, Dr Mockapetris deserves recognition as the man who, while working at the University of Southern California's Information Sciences Institute back in the early 1980s, came up with the system which provides the address architecture of the entire web.

The Domain Name System (DNS) developed by Mockapetris is crucial to how the net runs because it translates web address names, for example amazon.com or bbc.co.uk into numerical addresses that net routers can understand. DNS is essential for some key internet-based services such as applications from web searches and web mail to VoIP net phone calls.

Dr Mockapetris was also responsible for designing the first implementation of the internet's Simple Mail Transfer Protocol (SMTP) used for e-mail.

Reality check

Paul Mockapetris has made a crucial contribution to the development of the internet. At the same time, we need to recognize that, while the internet has come a long way in a short period of time, there is still much more to be done in terms of making the network both more useful and (critically) more secure.

E-bite

'The Domain Name System lies at the heart of every user experience with the internet.'

JENNIFER REXFORD, CHAIR OF ACM SIGCOMM.

Connectivity

The other major contributor to the technical development of the internet featured in this book is Tim Berners-Lee.

Potted biography

Paul Mockapetris is Chief Scientist at Nominum. He chaired the internet Engineering Task Force (IETF) from 1994 to 1996. In 2005, he was given an ACM Sigcomm lifetime award.

Sources and further reading

Paul Mockapetris, *Domain Name System,* Prentice Hall, 1994

26 Geoffrey A. Moore

Claim to fame

The man who conceived the Technology Adoption Life Cycle.

Writer and consultant Geoffrey Moore's Technology Adoption Life Cycle model – first unveiled in his book *Crossing the Chasm* – suggests that users of technology are 'distinguished from each other by their characteristic response to a discontinuous innovation based on a new technology'.

There are, according to Moore, five different categories that technology adopters can belong to, namely Innovators, Early Adopters, Early Majority, Late Majority and Laggards.

Moore sums them up as follows:

- **Innovators**: These are technology enthusiasts who pursue new products aggressively. They sometimes seek them out even before they have been launched. This is because technology is a central interest in their lives. There are not very many innovators in any given market segment, but winning them over at the outset of a marketing campaign is key nonetheless because their endorsement reassures the other players in the market place that the product does in fact work.
- **Early Adopters**: These are the visionaries who, like Innovators, buy into new product concepts very early in their life cycle, but unlike Innovators, they are not technologists. Rather they are people who find it easy to imagine, understand and appreciate the benefits of a new technology, and

to relate these potential benefits to their other concerns. Whenever they find a strong match, Early Adopters are willing to base their buying decisions upon it.

- **Early Majority**: These are pragmatists who share some of the Early Adopters' ability to relate to technology, but ultimately they are driven by a strong sense of practicality. They know that many of these new inventions end up as passing fads, so they are content to wait and see how other people are making out before they buy in themselves. Because there are so many people in this segment – roughly one-third of the whole adoption life cycle – winning their business is key to any substantial profits and growth.
- **Late Majority**: These people are conservative in outlook, sharing all the concerns of the Early Majority, plus one major additional one. Whereas people in the Early Majority feel able to handle a technology product, should they finally decide to purchase it, members of the Late Majority are not. As a result, they wait until something has become an established standard, and even then want to see lots of support before they buy, typically from large, well-established companies. Like the Early Majority, this group comprises about one-third of the total buying population in any given segment and so courting this group is highly profitable.
- **Laggards**: These are the sceptics who simply don't want anything to do with new technology for a variety of reasons, some personal and some economic. The only time they ever buy a technological product is when it is buried so deep inside another product – the way, say, that a microprocessor is designed into the braking system of a new car – that they don't even know it is there.

These profiles provide the foundation of Moore's second key model, the High-Tech Marketing Model. That model says that the way to develop a high-tech market is to focus initially on the Innovators, grow that market, then move on to the Early Adopters, grow that market, move on to the Early Majority, and so on through to the Late Majority, and even possibly to the Laggards. Companies, says Moore, need to use each 'captured' group as a base for creating momentum for marketing to the next group, i.e. the Innovators endorse a product and this becomes an important base from which a company can develop a credible pitch to the Early Adopters, the endorsement of the early adopters enables a pitch to the Early Majority, and so on.

There is a compelling business reason for keeping up the momentum, namely in Moore's words 'to take advantage of your day in the sun before the next day renders you obsolete'. Portable electric typewriters, for example, were displaced by portable PCs, which in turn may lose out at some point to internet terminals.

From this notion of having your day in the sun comes the idea of a *window of opportunity* – another of Moore's concepts for which he is rarely credited. If momentum is lost when a window of opportunity presents itself, then the chances are that a company will be overhauled by a competitor, 'thereby losing the advantages exclusive to a technology leadership position – specifically, the profit-margin advantage during the middle to late stages, which is the primary source from which high-tech fortunes are made'.

Reality check

The essence of the High-Tech Marketing Model is a smooth transition through all the stages of the Technology Adoption Life Cycle. For those companies that get it right, writes Moore, the potential rewards are huge: 'What is dazzling about this concept, particularly to those who own equity in a high-tech venture, is its promise of virtual monopoly over a major new market development. If you can get there first, 'catch the curve', and ride it up through the early majority segment, thereby establishing the de facto standard, you can get rich very quickly and 'own' a highly profitable market for a very long time to come.'

E-bite

'In high tech, the good news is that, although we lose our companies with alarming frequency, we keep the people along with the ideas, and so the industry as a whole goes forward vibrantly.'

TAKEN FROM *CROSSING THE CHASM: MARKETING AND SELLING PRODUCTS TO MAINSTREAM CUSTOMERS* BY GEOFFREY A. MOORE.

Potted biography

Geoffrey A. Moore is President of The Chasm Group, based in Palo Alto, California. The Chasm Group provides consultancy services to high-tech companies like Hewlett-Packard, Apple, PeopleSoft, AT&T, Oracle, Silicon Graphics and Sybase.

Connectivity

See Don Peppers and Martha Rogers for some practical tips about marketing using the internet.

Sources and further reading

Geoffrey A. Moore, *Crossing the Chasm: Marketing and Selling*

Technology Products to Mainstream Customers (2nd edn), HarperCollins, 1999

Geoffrey A. Moore, *Inside the Tornado,* HarperCollins, 1995

27 Gordon Moore

Claim to fame

Originator of Moore's Law.

Did you know that the computer in your mobile phone has more power than all the computers used during World War II combined? Or that a greeting card that plays Happy Birthday when you open it has more computing power than Apollo 11? Have you ever wondered why personal computers seem to go down in price and up in technical specification every year?

Behind all these 'interesting' facts is a phenomenon uncovered back in 1965 by Gordon Moore, when he was Director of Research and Development at Fairchild Semiconductor.

Moore had a paper published in *Electronics* magazine on April 19th, 1965 in which he wrote that 'the complexity for minimum component costs has increased at a rate of roughly a factor of two per year ... this rate can be expected to continue, if not to increase'. This observation was later tweaked to become a prediction that every 18 months or so, for the foreseeable future, chip density (and hence computing power) would double while cost remained constant, in effect creating ever more powerful computers without raising their price.

He based his prediction, which was to become known as Moore's Law, on his observation that his colleagues seemed to possess the ability to vastly decrease the size of semiconductors (or chips) with each succeeding generation of product. His investigations into the underlying physics of miniaturization determined that there was significant potential for this to continue for years.

Over the years, Moore's Law has held good. In fact, there are many industry commentators who believe that Moore's Law didn't simply describe a phenomenon – it actually became a self-fulfilling prophecy over time as the computer industry invested time, effort and money in keeping pace with Moore's prediction.

But no matter what has been driving this level of growth in computing power, the bottom line has been faster, cheaper, smaller computers.

Moore has been characteristically modest about the significance of his prediction. "If I hadn't published this paper in '65, the trends would have been obvious a decade later anyway. I don't think a particular paper made a difference. I was just in a position where I could see the trend," he one said in a newspaper interview.

Reality check

Moore's Law can be viewed as the first attempt at an algorithm to describe the accelerating progress of technology. Whereas Moore's forerunners, including writers like H. G. Wells, described technology as progressing on a linear scale, Moore planted the seed in people's minds that technology would grow exponentially.

E-bite

'Any exponential extrapolated far enough predicts disaster. The fact that materials are made of atoms will be a fundamental limit. We can't go smaller than that.'

GORDON MOORE, IN AN INTERVIEW CONDUCTED AT STANFORD UNIVERSITY.

Potted biography

Gordon Moore, now in his 70s, is currently Chairman Emeritus of Intel Corporation. In 1968 he co-founded Intel with Robert Noyce. He became President and Chief Executive Officer in 1975, holding that post until elected Chairman and Chief Executive Officer in 1979. He is a Director of Gilead Sciences Inc., a member of the National Academy of Engineering, and a Fellow of the IEEE. Moore also serves on the Board of Trustees of the California Institute of Technology. He received the National Medal of Technology from President George Bush in 1990. In 2000 he donated half his Intel stake to charity-environmental causes and education, including $300 million to his alma mater.

Connectivity

See also Robert Metcalfe for the second of the two most famous Laws driving the growth of the technology-based economy. For a more speculative view of where Moore's Law may lead us in the future, see Ray Kurzweil.

Sources and further reading

For a full transcript of the Stanford interview referred to above, go to www.stanford.edu/group/mmdd/SiliconValley/SiliconGenesis/GordonMoore/Moore.html

28 John Naisbitt

Claim to fame

Technology futurologist with the knack of being right.

John Naisbitt made his name with his book *Megatrends*, published in 1982. In it, Naisbitt examined the future impact of technology at a variety of levels – individual, organizational, societal and global. To read *Megatrends* again is to be reminded of just how profound and wide-ranging technological change has been over the past 25 years, the last five or so in particular.

In the book, John Naisbitt identified ten 'critical restructurings' that he believed would shape our lives. While some of his predictions have proved astonishingly accurate, others have either been wide off the mark or of diminishing significance.

Let's examine just four of his predictions from *Megatrends*:

- **Prediction**: *'Although we continue to think we live in an industrial society, we have in fact changed to an economy based on the creation and distribution of information.'*

  Comment: Through a 21st century lens, this statement appears self-evident. Twenty years ago, when the working population in the West was dominated by office workers and the manufacturing industry, it was a much bolder assertion.

- **Prediction**: *'No longer do we have the luxury of operating within an isolated, self-sufficient, national economic system; we must now acknowledge that we are part of a global economy… The* *bigger the world economy, the more powerful its smallest player.'*

Comment: The new economy is demonstrably a global economy. Thanks to internet technology, a one-person global business is both technically feasible and a practical reality.

- **Prediction**: *'In cities and states, in small organizations and subdivisions, we have rediscovered the ability to act innovatively and to achieve results from the bottom up.'*

  Comment: There is some evidence that grass roots groups – sometimes using the internet to co-ordinate efforts and to disseminate information instantaneously – are having some success. Within organizations, a combination of delayering and empowerment initiatives has devolved greater responsibility to those in the frontline.

- **Prediction**: *'From a narrow either/or society with a limited range of personal choices, we are exploding into a free-wheeling multiple option society.'*

  Comment: Perhaps for some, but certainly not for most people.

It's tempting to measure the value of *Megatrends* purely by the extent to which its predictions have come to pass. On that basis, in 1982 Naisbitt was able to come up with an impressively accurate foretaste of the e-business world, which he recognized would involve a combination of technology, e-business, free agent working and globalization.

Reality check

Critics of futurologists say that predicting the future is a sterile act that in itself makes nothing happen, any more than the act of betting influences which horse is first past the post. That assessment seems too harsh. Louis Pasteur once said that chance favors only the prepared-mind. By that token, characterizing the future helps in some measure to invent it.

E-bite

'The new source of power is not money in the hands of a few but information in the hands of many.'

'As the world becomes more universal, it also becomes more tribal. As people yield economic sovereignty and become economically interdependent, holding on to what distinguishes you from others becomes very important.'

JOHN NAISBITT, FROM HIS BOOK *GLOBAL PARADOX*, WILLIAM MORROW & COMPANY.

Potted biography

John Naisbitt (born 1930) worked as an executive with IBM and Eastman Kodak, and has been a distinguished international fellow at the Institute of Strategic and International Studies in Kuala Lumpur. He is a futurologist whose books have sold in their millions. Naisbitt was educated at Cornell.

Connectivity

For an insight into the thinking of a contemporary futurist, see Alvin Toffler.

Sources and further reading

John Naisbitt, *Megatrends*, Warner Books, 1982

John Naisbitt, Nana Naisbitt, & Douglas Philips, *High Tech High Touch*, Nicholas Brealey, 1999

John Naisbitt, *Global Paradox*

29 Nicholas Negroponte

Claim to fame

New economy commentator with a neat turn of phrase.

Founder and regular contributor to *Wired* magazine, Nicholas Negroponte is perhaps the world's best-known multi-media watcher and commentator. His book *Being Digital* was a bestseller when it first came out in 1995, confirming Negroponte at the time as one of the first and certainly one of the most readable trackers of the birth of the new economy.

In contrast to all too many e-business writers, Negroponte has a rare ability to distil complex phenomena into lucid prose, often using memorable language in the process. Probably his most widely quoted turn of phrase is one that he used to describe how the emphasis in world trade was increasingly shifting from physical transport to electronic transfer. As he put it in *Being Digital*:

> 'The best way to appreciate the merits and consequences of being digital is to reflect on the difference between atoms and bits. While we are undoubtedly in an information age, most information is delivered to us in the form of atoms: newspapers, magazines and books ... Our economy may be moving toward an information economy, but we measure trade and we write our balance sheets with atoms in mind.'

Negroponte certainly recognizes the value of conveying ideas in simple, memorable language. In his foreword to *Unleashing the Killer App* by Larry Downes and Chunka Mui, he reflected on his use of 'atoms' and 'bits':

> 'I comprehend something best when I can explain it in a few simple words. Describing the world in terms of 'bits and atoms,' as I did in my book *Being Digital*, provided those words. In fact, as a description of the digital world, the 'bits and atoms' distinction has improved, not weakened, over time. People quickly grasp the consequences of those Is and Os that have no weight, no size, no shape, and no color, and can travel at the speed of light.'

E-bite

"I'm angry with the likes of Microsoft and Apple. They've paid no attention to making computers easy to use. The problem with most computer companies is that they involve one geek making computer programs for another geek. There is nothing for the man on the street."

FROM A SPEECH GIVEN BY NEGROPONTE AT THE EDINBURGH TELEVISION FESTIVAL, AUGUST 1997.

Potted biography

Nicholas Negroponte is the Director of the Media Laboratory of the Massachusetts Institute of Technology, and is widely regarded as one of the world's leading experts on multimedia. He is also a founder of *Wired* magazine, to which he still regularly contributes.

Sources and further reading

Nicholas Negroponte, *Being Digital*, Knopf, 1995

30 Larry Page & Sergey Brin

Claim to fame

Founders of Google, the most used search engine on the planet.

In 1998, two young PhD students at Stanford University came up with an idea for an internet search engine and created a company called Google as a vehicle for developing and marketing their idea.

By June 2005, Google had become the world's biggest media company with an estimated stock market value of $80bn (£44bn) and around 3000 employees. Its dominant position in the search engine field is without question; when most people think search, they think Google. Most major dictionaries now feature 'google' as a verb.

Google has over eight billion pages of web-based information copied and indexed on its servers. Searches on Google are ranked by a complex formula which depend on a range of factors like popularity (the number of links from other sites) and the importance of referring sites (the BBC's, or The Washington Post's website, for example, carry more weight than a minor blog). Account is also taken of factors like font size and the location of a word on a page.

Google makes its money mainly from the small advertisements that appear alongside search results. The company now also sells advertising space to web publishers that is highly relevant to the page being viewed. So, for example, somebody searching for articles about cakes will see adverts for hand-crafted muffins and the like.

But Google is more than just a search engine. For example, the company set up an email service called Gmail recently. In 2005, products called Google Earth and Google Scholar (allowing users to search scientific, medical and technical journals) were launched.

We shouldn't be surprized that Google has diversified. In its stock market flotation documents, the company announced its intention to 'place smaller bets in areas that seem very speculative or even strange'. This apparently relentless flow of new products can be attributed in part to Google's practice of allowing its engineers to spend 20% of their time on any project that interests them.

E-bite

'Some say Google is God. Others say Google is Satan. But if they think Google is too powerful, remember that with search engines unlike other companies, all it takes is a single click to go to another search engine.'

SERGEY BRIN

Reality check

Google appears to reign supreme at the moment. But, like any technology company, it will need to keep an eye on Microsoft, which is currently ploughing hundreds of millions of dollars of research into search-related products. At its 2005 annual meeting, Microsoft Chief Executive Steve Ballmer declared ominously that "we will catch up and we will surpass Google."

However, perhaps the biggest threat to Google is its very success. The larger it gets, the more criticism it attracts. There are concerns about Google's objectivity and balance, given the power it has to influence what results are generated by searches. There are also a number of countries that have accused Google of cultural imperialism, in effect imposing an American world view.

Connectivity

Google changes the way we work and operate. The only other internet propositions that have approached this level of impact are Amazon and eBay, more on which can be found at Jeff Bezos and Meg Whitman.

Potted biographies

The son of a Michigan State University computer science professor, Larry Page's fascination with computers began at the age of six. He graduated from the University of Michigan, where he earned a BSc in Engineering. He then went to Stanford University, where he first met Sergey Brin. In 2002, Page was named a World Economic Forum Global Leader for Tomorrow. He was elected to the National Academy of Engineering in 2004.

Sergey Brin, a native of Moscow, received a BSc(Hons) in Mathematics and Computer Science from the University of Maryland at College Park. He is currently on leave from the PhD program in Computer Science at Stanford University, where he received his Masters. Brin has been a featured speaker at several international academic, business and technology forums, including the World Economic Forum and the Technology, Entertainment and Design Conference.

Sources and further reading

Neil Taylor, *Search Me: The Surprising Success of Google*, Cyan Books, 2005

John Battelle, *The Search: The Inside Story of How Google and Its Rivals Changed Everything*, Portfolio, 2005

31 Jeff Papows

Claim to fame

Ex-CEO of Lotus turns industry commentator.

As ex-CEO of Lotus – one of the best known and most progressive software companies – Jeff Papows has a decent vantage point from which to survey technology developments to date, which he describes as just 'really just a warm-up for the far greater changes to come.'

Businesses are going to have to change – and change radically – in order to compete effectively in the Web-based era: but the good news, says Papows, is that technological advances are opening as many windows of opportunity as they are threatening to close obsolete and outmoded ones.

Although he had proved to be an articulate and insightful commentator on developments in the technology field, what really interests Papows is the future, a future in which, for example, organizations will have to come to terms fully with the reality of a borderless, 24-hour world. He sees the inevitable rise of the 'market-facing enterprise,' with all relationships enhanced and even defined through technology.

Papows is astute enough to recognize that the future of information technology is relatively easy to predict compared to the many complex social, economic, cultural, and political variables that affect business evolution. We expect continuing powerful advances in technology – most of the other factors are far less predictable.

That said, for information technology to reach its full potential, many obstacles must be resolved in a timely and predictable manner. The greatest risks and challenges that lie ahead can, according to Papows writing in his book *Enterprise.com*, be divided into the following four areas:

1. **Technological and human limits**: 'It's nearly impossible to eliminate the risk that technology itself might not be able to deliver on the many promises it is making. Similarly, the demands of ever more sophisticated systems might one day outstrip the skills and talents of available workers.'

2. **Failed standards**: 'Even if the technological capacity exists, a real risk remains that today's rising levels of product interoperability will prove a temporary illusion. The IT industry has yet to prove in a systemic sense that its particular style of competition can sustain a meaningful 'open standards' process. The evidence of the last two years in this regard has been positive. But with the experience of the preceding two decades, there is every reason to be concerned that the industry dynamic could shift back to the direction of internecine warfare.'

3. **Lack of demand**: 'It's also perfectly possible that no matter what technologies and standards emerge, two further problems could arise: businesses might decide that there are limits to the value of automation, or consumers might decide that online services are simply not all that compelling. My personal sense on both counts is that the risk is fairly low; but with all our momentum and influence, it's critical that we never forget that it is the customer we must endeavor to satisfy, not ourselves.'

4. **Government intervention**: 'For reasons of commerce, culture, politics, fairness, and security, some governments may seek to block largely unfettered use of the internet. In this realm of internet governance, I can foresee two main problems: restrictions on the flow of commerce and restrictions on the flow of information.'

E-bite

'I learned in the Marines the price for being competitively wrong is, you're dead.'

JEFF PAPOWS

Reality check

Papows is a well-respected industry figure who offers us a detailed and thoughtful analysis of where business is headed over the next few years, but in truth his insights lack sparkle and originality. There's nothing wrong in what Papows is saying, and as a former major player in the software world, his views do carry considerable weight. Nonetheless, Papows tends to be somebody who consolidates and adds weight to views expressed by others rather than a true original in his own right.

Connectivity

Papows is now one of the elder statesmen of the technology industry. For another 'wise head' view, check out Peter Drucker.

Potted biography

Jeff Papows is President and CEO of Lotus Development Corporation based in Cambridge, Massachusetts. A prominent voice in the information technology industry, he is a frequent commentator in the business media and a regular keynote speaker at conferences. He holds a PhD.

Sources and further reading

Jeff Papows, *Enterprise.com*, Nicholas Brealey, 1999

32 Don Peppers & Martha Rogers

Claim to fame

Top-notch marketers who understand how IT impacts on the marketing process.

Most companies, and certainly those with an intuitive grasp of how the e-business world is unfolding, know that customers are no longer passive recipients of a service or purchasers of a product. Customers tell you what they want, and expect you to fit around their needs and circumstances. They expect you to remember them. And as for the idea that, once with you, they will stay for life, the 21st century customer's attitude is 'If you want loyalty, get a dog'.

Against this backdrop, companies are coming to recognize that they need to listen to customers far more attentively and, above all else, recognize that customers come in packages of one.

Writers and consultants Don Peppers and Martha Rogers believe that information technology is making three important new capabilities available to businesses:

- Powerful databases that enable the company to tell their customers apart and remember them individually.
- Interactivity, which means that the customer can now talk to the company directly.
- Mass customization technology that enables businesses to customize products and services as a matter of routine.

But the challenge of putting in place a successful mass customization program goes far deeper than buying the right IT solution. Assuming a company can harness the information technology needed and put in place an appropriately skilled and motivated workforce, there still needs to be a well-developed and executed marketing strategy to ensure that, alongside the needs of individual customers, the company's financial needs are being met. There is no corporate merit to brilliantly serving inherently unprofitable customers and going into receivership.

From a strategic and financial perspective, therefore, companies need to use information generated about customers to identify their value to the business. In their book *Enterprise One-to-One*, Peppers and Rogers write that 'a customer's lifetime value (LTV) will depend largely on how long the customer remains loyal, and even small increases in the rate of customer retention add significantly to LTV'.

Knowing what different customers need, however, involves much more than simply keeping a record of what they've bought. Companies need increasingly to know why. This is important because two customers might buy the same product for quite different reasons; knowing the thinking behind the purchase gives a company a much better chance of securing future business.

While customers with the highest lifetime values are the ones you most want to nurture and retain, Peppers and Rogers suggest that second-tier customers – customers who don't have as high an actual valuation – are likely to have the most potential for growth. Keeping a first-tier customer will usually involve different strategies from those needed for growing a second-tier customer. At the other end of the spectrum, most companies also have a bottom rung of customers who are, for all practical purposes, of no value to the company. Shaking off these customers is not easy: taking positive action to do so can attract negative publicity as Barclays Bank discovered when it closed down a number of its rural branches in the UK in the early part of 2000.

E-bite

'Speed and good communications are essential if mass customization is to work. Get them right, and another prize is yours. In Henry Ford's day, Ford made the car and the customer paid for it. in Michael Dell's day, the customer pays for the computer and then Dell makes it.'

TAKEN FROM *ENTERPRISE ONE-TO-ONE: TOOLS FOR COMPETING IN THE INTERACTIVE AGE* BY DON PEPPERS AND MARTHA ROGERS.

Reality check

Nine years or so after its publication, *Enterprise One-to-One* remains about the best book around about how customers and companies will interact in the new economy. It's a book that achieves the rare distinction of offering both a strategic perspective and a set of practical tools and tips whilst being absolutely convincing at both levels. Most critical of all, they leave the reader in no doubt that, just as mass production transformed manufacturing in the 20th century, so mass customization is set to be just as significant in the 21st century.

E-bite

'When you subscribe to a new magazine, the first year might cost $35.90 but the second year the price is $75.90. Why? Because presumably you like the magazine. Charging regular customers more is a natural consequence of trying to acquire new customers by using discounts, and virtually every business tries to do it. But by tailoring a product to a customer's individual specifications, and then constantly upgrading the product to match the customer's needs better and better, the enterprise can establish a Learning Relationship with the customer. Over time, the enterprise not only makes the customer more and more loyal, it increases its own value to that customer – as every interaction leads to a better tailored service or product.'

TAKEN FROM *ENTERPRISE ONE-TO-ONE.*

Connectivity

For another view of the internet from a marketing perspective, have a look at Geoffrey Moore, whose Technology Adoption Life Cycle is an illuminating model.

Potted biographies

Don Peppers and Martha Rogers are authors of a number of best-selling business books, most of them based around their concept of 'one-to-one marketing.' Their company, the Peppers and Rogers Group, offers consulting and training in customer relationship management, and has featured in the Inc 500 list of the fastest growing companies in the US.

Sources and further reading

Don Peppers & Martha Rogers, *Enterprise One-to-One: Tools for Competing in the Interactive Age,* Doubleday, 1997

Don Peppers, Martha Rogers, & Bob Dorf, *The One- to-One Fieldbook,* Doubleday, 1999

33 Michael Porter

> **Claim to fame**
>
> Business strategy guru who debunked such internet myths as first-mover advantage and the power of virtual companies.

Michael Porter is just about the most pre-eminent name in the strategic planning field. There probably isn't an MBA student in the world who isn't familiar with Porter's 'Five Forces' Model and his generic competitive strategies.

Many have argued that the introduction of the internet into business practices renders advocates of the old rules of strategy and sustainable competitive advantage like Porter irrelevant.

Not surprisingly, Porter doesn't subscribe to this view. In a 2001 *Harvard Business Review* article called *Strategy and the Internet,* he writes that 'the only way (for companies to be more profitable than the average performer) is by achieving a sustainable competitive edge – by operating at a lower cost, by commanding a premium price, or by doing both'.

The internet tends to weaken industry profitability without providing proprietary operational advantages, Porter believes that it is more important than ever for companies to distinguish themselves through strategy. The winners will be those that view the internet as a complement to, not a cannibal of, traditional ways of competing.

Many of the early internet pioneers, both the newly minted dot.coms and those well-established companies seeking an online presence, have competed in ways that violate nearly every principle in the strategy rule book. As Porter puts it: 'Rather than focus on profits, they have chased customers indiscriminately through discounting, channel incentives, and advertising. Rather than concentrate on delivering value that earns an attractive price from customers, they have pursued indirect revenues such as advertising and click-through fees. Rather than make trade-offs they have rushed to offer every conceivable product or service'.

On the back of these misconceived strategies, many a dot.com crumpled and folded. The good news, says Porter, is that it did not have to be this way. These were bad strategic choices but they were not the only options available. And these choices had little to do with the inherent business potential of the internet.

In fact, when it comes to reinforcing a distinctive strategy, Porter maintains that the internet provides a better technological platform than any previous generation of IT.

For most existing industries and established companies, the internet rarely cancels out important sources of competitive advantage: if anything, it is more likely to increase the value of those sources. But over time, says Porter, the internet itself will be neutralized as a source of advantage as all companies embrace its technology.

E-bite

'In periods of transition such as the one we have been going through, it often appears as if there are new rules of competition. But as market forces play out, as they are now, the old rules regain their currency. The creation of true economic value once again becomes the final arbiter of business success.'

MICHAEL PORTER, WRITING IN *HARVARD BUSINESS REVIEW*, MARCH 2001.

Reality check

Gaining competitive advantage in the post-internet business world does not require a radically new approach to business; and it certainly does not require the abandonment of classic economic principles that can still offer strategic value in a market place that depends on cutting-edge information technology.

No, gaining competitive advantage in the early years of the 21st century is still reliant on applying proven principles of effective strategy as set out by Porter in *Competitive Strategy*. Sources of strategic advantage rest where they always have – in cost competitiveness, product differentiation, ease of entering and exiting markets, and so on.

Potted biography

Born in 1947, and a Former Captain of the US Army Reserve, Michael Porter gained an MBA with high distinction in 1971 from Harvard Business School. He subsequently taught at Harvard, becoming only the fourth member of the School ever to be honoured with the title of University Professor. His 1980 book *Competitive Strategy,* written when he was in his early thirties, is now in its 53rd printing and has been translated into 17 languages.

Connectivity

Andy Grove has taken some of Porter's ideas and projected them into the context of the internet economy.

Sources and further reading

Michael Porter, *Competitive Strategy,* Free Press, 1980

Michael Porter, *Strategy and the Internet,* Harvard Business Review, March 2001

Michael Porter, *What is Strategy,* Harvard Business Review, November-December 1996

34 David S. Pottruck and Terry Pearce

Claim to fame

Early pioneers of the view that a successful e-business needs great technology **and** great people.

At a time when internet businesses all have access to similar technology, and when the models for online businesses are such that they can be copied readily, often within a matter of days, how can they achieve a sustainable advantage over their rivals?

The answer, say Pottruck and Pearce, both senior players in the Charles Schwab Corporation, lies in that often overlooked resource – people. Not just ordinary people, but those with passion. Passionate companies have cultures that are intentionally created and sustained, and which unequivocally support individual contribution, teamwork, and risk-taking. Business practices in passionate organizations are anchored in the principles that helped the company become successful in the first place. Because of this, passionate companies are more likely to have passionate leaders on board who are themselves driven by a strong set of values, coupled with a genuine desire for their organization and the people who work there to succeed.

Pottruck and Moore's advocacy of passion is not simply the result of a random outbreak of touchy-feeliness. Underpinning the idea is some fundamentally sound internet business logic. Here's how the they explain it in their book *Clicks and Mortar*:

> 'Technological doors have opened wide to a new global, electronic economy. But the new economy is not built simply on fast distribution of information. This new economy is built upon a central premise of continuous change. In other words, we the people have to create new information: ideas that have not been thought of before. Thus the new economy rewards constant improvement and innovation, and these are derived from the minds and imaginations of people. To compete, we have to innovate faster than the next guy – who is trying to do the same thing. And of course, the next guy is no longer just in the office building across the street or across town but could be anywhere, in any garage or carriage-house, in just about any country in the world.'

Reality check

Passion plus technology is an equation that demonstrably can work. The fact that the authors employed these principles and ideas during their involvement in the meteoric rise of the Charles Schwab Corporation is a clear indication that their ideas have value. What is most striking is Pottruck and Moore's absolute faith that, in any business endeavour – be it clicks or bricks – the difference that makes the difference is the centrality of the human heart.

E-bite

'With results measured quarter to quarter and competitive pressures demanding ever-faster decisions, any practice that sounds like it will slow things down feels antithetical to business success. Any principle that requires an attention to process, such as culture building, can seem useless. Building and reinforcing culture takes time, lots of it, and it can seem like a waste or a luxury in a world with a premium on speed.

'But ignoring cultural construction breeds discontent and actually slows progress. Investing time in alignment is like tuning an engine; it creates efficiency that will not only pay off in results, it will make the whole journey smoother and more fulfilling.'

TAKEN FROM *CLICKS AND MORTAR: PASSION DRIVEN GROWTH WORLD* BY DAVID S. POTTRUCK AND TERRY PEARCE.

Connectivity

For another human-centred view of how the internet works, see Gerry McGovern.

Potted biographies

David S. Pottruck is President and co-CEO of the Charles Schwab Corporation. Terry Pearce is President of Leadership Communication, and an Executive Communications Officer at Schwab. He also teaches at the Haas School of Business at the University of California, Berkeley.

Sources and further reading

David S. Pottruck & Terry Pearce, *Clicks and Mortar: Passion Driven Growth in an Internet Driven World,* Jossey Bass, 2000

Edgar H Schein, *Organizational Culture and Leadership,* Jossey-Bass, 1992.

Highly recommended for those who want to take their exploration of organizational culture further.

35 Thomas Stewart

Claim to fame

Early populariser of the intellectual capital concept.

There was a time when capital assets could be viewed in purely financial or physical terms – they showed up in the buildings and equipment owned, it could be found in the corporate balance sheets. In the knowledge economy, however, there exists a rather more elusive form of asset: intellectual capital.

In his book *Intellectual Capital,* Thomas Stewart provides a practical guide to the significance of intellectual capital, which he defines as 'packaged useful knowledge'.

According to Stewart, intellectual capital can be broken down into three areas:

1. **Human capital**: The knowledge that resides within the heads of employees that is relevant to the purpose of the organization. Human capital is formed and deployed, writes Stewart, 'when more of the time and talent of the people who work in a company is devoted to activities that result in innovation'. Human capital can grow in two ways, 'when the organization uses more of what people know, and when people know more stuff that is useful to the organization'. Unleashing the human capital resident in the organization requires 'minimizing mindless tasks, meaningless paperwork, unproductive infighting'.

2. **Customer capital**: The value of a company's ongoing relationships with the people or organizations to which it sells. Indicators of customer capital include market share, customer retention and defection rates, and profit per customer. Stewart's belief is that 'customer capital is probably – and startlingly when you think about it – the worst managed of all intangible assets. Many businesses don't even know who their customers are'.
3. **Structural capital**: The knowledge retained within the organization that becomes company property. Stewart calls this 'knowledge that doesn't go home at night'. Structural capital 'belongs to the organization as a whole. It can be reproduced and shared'. Examples of structural capital include technologies, inventions, publications and business processes.

Reality check

Understanding what intellectual capital amounts to is only part of the story for organizations. The true value comes in being able to capture and deploy it. To this end, Stewart came up with the following ten principles in his book for managing intellectual capital:

1. Companies don't own human and customer capital. Only by recognizing the shared nature of these assets can a company manage and profit from these assets.
2. To create human capital that it can use, a company needs to foster teamwork, communities of practice and other social forms of learning.
3. Organizational wealth is created around skills and talents that are proprietary and scarce. To manage and develop human capital companies must recognize unsentimentally that people with these talents are assets to invest in. Others are costs to be minimized.

4. Structural assets (those intangible assets the company owns) are the easiest to manage but those that customers care least about.
5. Move from amassing knowledge just-in-case to having information that customers need ready-to-hand, and that which they might need within reasonable reach.
6. Information and knowledge can, and should, substitute for expensive physical and financial assets.
7. Knowledge work is custom work.
8. Every company should re-analyze the value chain of the industry that it participates in to see what information is most crucial.
9. Focus on the flow of information not the flow of materials.
10. Human, structural and customer capital work together. It is not enough to invest in people, systems and customers separately. They can support each other or detract from each other.

E-bite

'Knowledge assets, like money or equipment, exist and are worth cultivating only in the context of strategy. You cannot define and manage intellectual assets unless you know what you want to do with them.'

THOMAS STEWART, *INTELLECTUAL CAPITAL*

Connectivity

For a better understanding of the origins of the knowledge economy, see Peter Drucker.

Potted biography

Thomas A. Stewart is a member of the board of editors of *Fortune* magazine. He pioneered the field of intellectual capital in a series of articles that earned him an international reputation, the Planning Forum calling him 'the leading proponent of knowledge management in the business press'. He lives in Manhattan.

Sources and further reading

Thomas A. Stewart, *Intellectual Capital: The New Wealth of Organizations*, Doubleday, 1997

Thomas A Stewart, *The Wealth of Knowledge*, Nicholas Brealey, 2001

36 Alvin Toffler

Claim to fame

Futorologist who correctly predicted the impact of technology in the 21st century.

The 'Third Wave' referred to in the title of Alvin Toffler's 1980 classic is the age of 'the super-industrial society' in which the new technologies redefine how people operate at a societal, organizational and personal level.

Following two preceding waves (the agricultural phase of civilization's development and then the 'Second Wave' of industrialization), the Third Wave, Toffler anticipated, would bring with it much anxiety, trauma and uncertainty.

'Old ways of thinking,' he wrote, 'old formulas, dogmas, and ideologies, no matter how cherished or how useful in the past, no longer fit the facts... The world that is fast emerging from the clash of new values and technologies, new geopolitical relationships, new lifestyles and modes of communication, demands wholly new ideas and analogies, classifications and concepts'.

So how does Toffler's view of the future compare to what has actually unfolded over the past 25 years?

Pretty well in the main. For example, Toffler wrote that 'the essence of Second Wave manufacture was the long 'run' of millions of identical standardized products. By contrast, the essence of Third Wave manufacture is the short run of partially or completely customized products'.

This prediction was spot on. Mass production has indeed increasingly yielded pride of place to the concept of mass customization, to the extent that the latter now dominates most traditional mass production industries such as car manufacture.

He also predicted that the customer will become 'so integrated into the production process that we will find it more and more difficult to tell just who is actually the consumer and who the producer'. Again, Toffler has been proved correct. Online banking services, and Amazon's customers contributing book reviews are just two examples where customers now routinely do 'work' on behalf of companies they deal with.

Elsewhere he correctly predicted cultural fragmentation, the shift to a global economy, the flattening of organizational hierarchies, corporate downsizing, house-husbands, the demise of the job for life, and portfolio working inter alia.

In more recent years, his focus has been on the increasing power of 21st century military hardware, weapons and technology proliferation.

Reality check

Reading *The Third Wave* over a quarter of a century after its first publication is a curious experience. On one hand, the book remains very contemporary in feel, and his profile of the e-business is a pretty close match. On the other hand, when he gets down to the level of describing the nuts and bolts of technology to come, the book seems remarkably dated. For example, at one point he goes into some detail to describe a word processor. Perhaps though that should merely serve to remind us how rapidly wave upon wave of technological innovation has come at us. *The Third Wave* has proved to be a largely accurate depiction of a future that has now more or less reached us. Given the status it has achieved, it seems all the more remarkable that it is currently virtually impossible to locate a copy in a bookstore – either bricks-and-mortar or on-line. Maybe the future isn't what it used to be.

Potted biography

Alvin Toffler was born in the US in 1928. A former Washington correspondent and editor of *Fortune* magazine, Alvin Toffler is a highly respected futurologist. He has briefly served as a visiting professor at Cornell University and a visiting scholar at the Russell Sage Foundation. He holds a number of honorary degrees.

E-bite

'The illiterate of the 21st century will not be those who cannot read and write, but those who cannot learn, unlearn, and relearn.'

ALVIN TOFFLER, *FUTURE SHOCK*

Connectivity

Toffler's view of the future was largely formed in the 1970s and 1980s and his value lies in the fact that much of what he predicted has come to pass. Have a look at Ray Kurzweil for a challenging view of technology in years to come.

Sources and further reading

Alvin Toffler, *The Third Wave*, Bantam, 1980

Alvin Toffler, *Future Shock*, Bantam, 1970

37 Linus Torvalds

Claim to fame

Creator of the Linux operating system.

Linus (pronounced LEE-nus) Torvalds is the Finnish software innovator who, while still studying at the University of Helsinki, created an operating system called Linux.

Having designed what many industry players reckon to be a much better operating system than Microsoft's, Torvalds spurned the opportunity to secure the patents and intellectual rights that would have guaranteed him a personal fortune. Instead, he decided to release details of the internal workings of Linux on the internet for free.

By doing this, he became perhaps the most significant contributor to a growing open access movement, a movement in which thousands of fellow programers from all around the world contribute their brainpower and experience to rewriting online the software code that drives computer programs.

This approach has worked well for Torvalds. The estimated 10m or so users of Linux consider it far superior to any other Unix software, precisely because it is continuously improved by the work of collective minds.

It is a testament to the power of this process, and to Torvald's original work that Linux has now become a powerful brand recognized by Microsoft and others as a significant source of competition.

E-bite

'Microsoft isn't evil, they just make really crappy operating systems.'

LINUS TORVALDS

Reality check

Windows and Linux have both enjoyed success in recent years because both systems run on machines using low-cost PCs, thus enabling companies to trim large sums off their IT operating costs.

Because of the growing perception that Linux is a better product than Windows, industry analysts believe that Linux and its open-source cousins could significantly batter Microsoft's profit margins and growth over the coming years.

This is in part because Microsoft is unsure about how to deal with this highly unconventional rival. In most market places, Microsoft has been able to gain supremacy by adopting a high-volume, low-cost strategy. Open-source software is a bottom-up, collaborative phenomenon, providing a very different kind of competitor for Bill Gates and his team.

Potted biography

Born in Helsinki in 1969, Linus Torvalds studied Computer Science at the University of Helsinki. In 1997, Torvalds moved to California to join Transmeta, a start-up company in the first stages of designing an energy saving Central Processing Unit (CPU). In 2003, Linus left Transmeta in order to focus exclusively on developing Linux and to begin working under the auspices of the Open Source Development Labs (OSDL) a consortium formed by high tech companies including IBM,

Hewlett-Packard, Intel, AMD, RedHat, Novell and many others. The purpose of the consortium is to promote Linux development.

Connectivity

For more on Microsoft's view of the world, see Bill Gates. For another example of how an iconoclast can change the competitive rules of the game, have a look at Niklas Zennstrom for more on how Skype is shaking up the telephony industry.

Sources and further reading

Linus Torvalds et al., *Just for Fun: The Story of an Accidental Revolutionary,* HarperBusiness, 2001

Pekka Himanen, *The Hacker Ethic and the Spirit of the Information Age,* Secker and Warburg, 2001

38 Meg Whitman

Claim to fame

CEO of eBay – one of the world's most successful internet business.

On an average day, there are millions of items listed on eBay. People come to eBay to buy and sell items in thousands of categories from collectibles like trading cards, antiques, dolls, and housewares through to practical items like used cars, clothing, books and CDs, and electronics.

In 2005, there were around 150 million registered users and the company had revenues of around $4 billion. The company accounts for about one quarter of all e-commerce sales in the US, excluding groceries and travel.

As President and CEO of eBay since March 1998, Meg Whitman has led the company to become the number one consumer e-commerce site. Her expertise in brand building, combined with her consumer technology experience, has helped eBay evolve into a leading company that is reshaping how commerce takes place around the world.

eBay is a true peer-to peer model. It facilitates direct exchanges between people who go to its site to list products for sale or to search listings of products for sale. The actual exchange takes place between individuals. Just as (music file-swapping company) Napster provides a central file directory that allows individuals to swap songs, eBay provides a central listing that allows individuals to buy and sell merchandise. As with Napster, the network members can act as either distributor or consumer.

In essence, eBay makes its money by providing a technology platform that enables users to interact with each other and then skims money off every transaction. This model, like the demand-aggregation models of other e-pioneers, moves from a fixed 'take it or leave it' price determined by sellers (and based most often on cost) to a variable price that actually reflects the true value to the customer as determined by the customers that bid for them.

E-bite

'A business leader has to keep their organization focused on the mission. That sounds easy, but it can be tremendously challenging in today's competitive and ever-changing business environment. A leader also has to motivate potential partners to join.'

MEG WHITMAN

Reality check

When eBay increased its fees sharply in January 2005, many of its registered sellers complained, their sense of grievance exacerbated by a feeling that eBay was to all intents a monopoly. Meg Whitman was dismissive of the idea that users had nowhere else to go, but the reality is that no other online auction site comes anywhere near the size, scope and sheer market presence of eBay.

That said, eBay's future competition is less likely to come from one major competitor, and will more probably stem from hundreds, if not thousands, of people setting up and selling from their own websites and using various marketing devices to promote themselves.

Potted biography

Margaret C. Whitman, more widely known as Meg Whitman, was born in 1956. She studied at Princeton, graduating with an Economics degree in 1977, before taking an MBA at Harvard. Her career took her to a range of companies including Procter & Gamble, Bain and Company, the Walt Disney Corporation and Hasbro Inc. She has been President and CEO of the online auction company eBay since March 1998. *Time* magazine named her one of the world's 100 most influential people in 2004 and 2005, and *Fortune* magazine ranked her the most powerful woman in American business in 2004.

Connectivity

Whitman attributes much of eBay's success to its willingness to follow the pointers provided by its customers. For more on the value of placing customer desires at the centre of things, see Regis McKenna and Don Peppers and Martha Rogers.

Sources and further reading

Meg and the Power of Many, The Economist, June 9th 2005

Adam Cohen, *The Perfect Store: Inside EBay,* Piatkus Books, 2003

39 Niklas Zennström

Claim to fame

The man behind the latest next big thing – VOIP.

'I knew it was over when I downloaded Skype,' Michael Powell, Chairman of the Federal Communications Commission in the US, admitted in an interview that appeared in *Fortune* magazine in 2004. 'When the inventors of KaZaA are distributing for free a little program that you can use to talk to anybody else, and the quality is fantastic, and it's free – it's over. The world will change now inevitably.'

Niklas Zennström, CEO and co-founder with Janus Friis of a company called Skype, has been described as a quiet iconoclast. Zennström initially caught the eye as one of the people behind KaZaA, a piece of software that enabled millions of music lovers to illegally download songs.

With his latest venture, he is not offering the world free illegal music but free and entirely legal global telephony. The rapid proliferation of broadband, plus Skype, gives us a real choice in communications. Using a system called Voipm (short for Voice Over Internet Protocol), Skype allows users to make free, unlimited calls via their internet. All that is needed is a PC microphone and speakers, or an affordable PC headset.

E-bite

'The idea of charging for calls belongs to the last century. Skype software gives people new power to affordably stay in touch with their friends and family by taking advantage of their technology and connectivity investments.'

NIKLAS ZENNSTRÖM, QUOTED ON THE SKYPE WEBSITE

Reality check

It's no exaggeration to say that, with the arrival of Skype, the telecom industry will never be the same. Since its launch in 2004, Skype has attracted over 40 million users.

There is a cloud on the horizon, however. Skype's software is a proprietary standard whereas rival file-sharing networks are based on open standards, a more popular option for many. Because Skype is so far incompatible with a standard (called SIP) used by rival internet-telephony operators, it may turn out that, as with KaZaA, Zennström has put his finger on an important trend, but that his software will not ultimately prevail.

Connectivity

For more on how a new breed of internet upstart is changing the rules of the game, go to Linus Torvalds.

Potted biography

Niklas Zennström, a Swedish citizen, has a business degree and an MSc in Engineering Physics gained from Uppsala University in Sweden. He co-founded and served as CEO of KaZaA, after that he founded Joltid, a software company developing and marketing peer-to-peer (p2p) solutions and technologies to companies. His latest venture Skype, a global internet telephony company founded in 2003, is based on peer-to-peer principles.

Sources and further reading

The Quiet Iconoclast, The Economist, July 1st 2004

Fortune magazine, February 16th 2004

40 Shoshana Zuboff

Claim to fame

Harvard professor who raises profound questions about the impact of IT.

Can a Harvard professor whose main claim to fame is a book about technology written in the 1980s, and based on research conducted up to a decade before, tell us anything about business life in the 21st century?

The answer is yes – because Shoshana Zuboff's *In the Age of the Smart Machine* is a real rarity – a nearly 20 year old technology classic. Zuboff achieves this feat by concentrating less on the technology itself and more on its meaning and potential in business life.

Picking through the book brings out a number of key themes, most of which still have great relevance today. For example, she was one of the first people to identify the potential of information technology to transform work at every organizational level by having the potential to give all workers, regardless of hierarchical status, a comprehensive or near comprehensive view of the entire business.

She also observed how information technologies potentially increase the intellectual content of work at all levels and thus present organizations with a stark choice: do we use IT to continue automation at the risk of robbing workers of gratification and self image, or to empower ordinary working people to make judgments?

Zuboff is in no doubt about the answer, believing that to unlock the promise of information technology, organizational leaders must be prepared to dismantle managerial hierarchies that all too often block the ready flow of information.

Reality check

As with the original Industrial Revolution, there are bound to be winners and losers from the introduction of information technologies. For every empowered, delayered, nanotechnology worker doing valuable work, there is another who has lost their job, and yet another tucked away in their technologically Neanderthal office putting in longer and longer hours doing more of the same work. Are we destined to live in a world where some people are permanently overworked while others are permanently underworked?

E-bite

'The informated organization is a learning institution, and one of its principal purposes is the expansion of knowledge – not knowledge for its own sake (as in academic pursuit), but knowledge that comes to reside at the core of what it means to be productive. Learning is no longer a separate activity that occurs either before one enters the workplace or in remote classroom settings. Nor is it an activity preserved for a managerial group. The behaviors that define learning and the behaviors that define being productive are one and the same. Learning is not something that requires time out from being engaged in productive activity; learning is the heart of productive activity. To put it simply, learning is the new form of labor.'

TAKEN FROM *IN THE AGE OF THE SMART MACHINE: THE FUTURE OF WORK AND POWER* BY SHOSHANA ZUBOFF

Potted biography

Shoshana Zuboff is a Professor at the Harvard Business School. She has written extensively about how computers will affect the future of work.

Connectivity

For more on how the internet redefines work practices, see Peter Drucker and Kevin Kelly.

Sources and further reading

Shoshana Zuboff, *In the Age of the Smart Machine: the Future of Work and Power*, Basic Books, 1988

Shoshana Zuboff, *The Emperor's New Workplace*, Scientific American, September 1995

FIVE
Case studies

In this section, we will look at a number of organizations and how they tackled – with varying levels of success – challenges facing their businesses. Each case study will be followed by a brief outline of key lessons or insights to be drawn.

The companies featured are as follows:

1. Dell Computer Corporation
2. Encyclopaedia Britannica
3. Seven-Eleven
4. Vermeer Technologies

Dell Computer Corporation

"It's easy to fall in love with how far you've come and how much you've done. It's definitely harder to see the cracks in a structure you've built yourself, but that's all the more reason to look hard and look often. Even if something seems to be working, it can be improved."

MICHAEL DELL, CEO, DELL COMPUTER CORPORATION

The organization

By the age of 12, Michael Dell's entrepreneurial streak was beginning to emerge. That year, he earned $2,000 from selling stamps. By the time he was 18, he was selling customized personal computers. He started the Dell Computer Corporation in 1984 with $1,000, dropping out of his Biology course at Austin University in Texas. The company, under his leadership, has gone on to become one of the most successful computer businesses in the world, redefining the industry with its direct-sale approach and the customer support model it pioneered. Dell himself is a member of the Board of Directors of the United States Chamber of Commerce and the Computer-world/Smithsonian Awards.

The story

Dell Computer Corporation is one of the computer industry's biggest success stories. Established in 1984, Michael Dell founded his company with the unprecedented idea of bypassing the middleman and selling custom-built computers direct to end users. His premise from the beginning was to under-promise and over-deliver – and that applied to customers, suppliers and employees alike.

Originally an 'offline' business, Dell was quick to appreciate the potential of the internet – in fact, he built an e-business before anyone had even coined the term. Dell.com was a natural extension of the offline business. The site is customer, rather than product, focused, being aligned by customer categories, not hardware model lines. The site directs the different type of customers to a second-level page, where the relevant line of Dell products is presented.

Pursuing this customer orientation still further, Dell brings customers into the product-planning and manufacturing processes, not just the sales process, and management encourages everyone in the company to have contact with customers.

Here's how Michael Dell himself characterizes his business approach in his book *Direct from Dell*:

- **Think about the customer, not the competition**: Competitors represent your industry's past, as, over the years, collective habits become ingrained. Customers are your future, representing new opportunities, ideas and avenues for growth.

- **Work to maintain a healthy sense of urgency and crisis**: This doesn't mean that you want to fabricate deadlines or keep people so stressed that they quickly burn out. Set the bar slightly higher than you normally would, so that your people can achieve aggressive goals by working smarter.
- **Be opportunistic, but also be fast**: Look to find opportunity, especially when it isn't readily apparent. Focusing on the customer doesn't mean that you should ignore the competition. If something that your competition did or didn't do provided you with an opportunity today, would you recognize it and be able to act on it immediately? Today a competitive win can literally be decided one day at a time. You have to act fast, be ready, then be ready to change – fast.
- **Be the hunter, not the hunted**: Success is a dangerous thing, as we are at once invincible and vulnerable. Always strive to keep your team focused on growing the business and on winning and acquiring new business. Even though your company may be leading the market, you never want your people to act as though you are. That leads to complacency, and complacency kills. Encourage people to think, 'This is good. This worked. Now how can we take what we've proven and rise it to win new business?' There's a big difference between asking that and asking, 'How can we defend our existing accounts?'

Analysis

Obsessive customer focus linked to strategic savvy and an ongoing commitment to innovation are clearly instrumental to Dell's success over the years, but just as important has been Michael Dell's commitment to internal organizational processes.

He has described culture as 'one of the most enigmatic facets of management' that he has encountered 'and also one of the most important."'

When asked which of his competitors represented the biggest threat to Dell, he said that the greatest threat wouldn't come from a competitor, it would come from the people who worked for Dell. His goal at Dell has been to make sure that everybody at Dell feels they are a part of 'something great – something special – perhaps something even greater than themselves'. To achieve this, he set out from the beginning to create a company of owners. As he puts it in *Direct from Dell*:

> 'Creating a culture in which every person in your organization, at every level, thinks and acts like an owner means that you need to aim to connect individual performance with your company's most important objectives. For us, that means we mobilize everyone around creating the best possible customer experience and enhancing shareholder value – and we use specific quantifiable measurements of our progress towards those goals that apply to every employee's performance. A company composed of individual owners is less focused on hierarchy and who has the nicest office, and more intent on achieving their goals.'

Simply put, Dell's approach is about establishing and maintaining a healthy, competitive culture by partnering with his people through shared objectives and a common strategy.

This is not just a lofty statement; it is backed up by a set of highly practical actions. When recruiting, for example, the company looks for people who are completely in synch with its business philosophy and objectives. Dell says: 'If the person thinks in a way that's compatible with your company values and beliefs, and understands what the company does and is driven to do, he will not only work hard to fulfil his immediate goals, but he will also contribute to the greater goals of the organization.' That's not to say that Dell encourages 'herd' thinking – but that everyone in the company is mobilized around a customer-oriented focus.

Because of the constant demand for talent, recruiting is a non-stop, year-round activity, like R&D or sales. The result is a steady pipeline of talent. Dell doesn't recruit strictly for job openings: it hires the best available candidates, even if that means creating a new position. To quote Andy Esparza, the company's Head of Staffing, 'Why would you choose not to hire a great person just because there's no job opening at the present time?'

Dell Computers then has an intensely people-centric culture. For any company that wishes to emulate the Dell model, there seem to be six keys to their approach. These can be summed up as follows:

1. Mobilize your people around a common goal.
2. Invest in long-term goals by hiring ahead of the game and communicating this commitment to your people.
3. Don't leave the talent search to the human resources section – get personally involved as much as you can.
4. Cultivate a commitment to personal growth.
5. Build an infrastructure that rewards mastery – the best way to keep talented people is to allow their jobs to change with them.
6. Keep in touch with people at all levels of the company – immerse yourself in real information with real people

The section will conclude with a feature called something like *Best Practice: pulling it all together,* in which I will look at what can we conclude from the case studies in this section.

e-Bay

The business model of eBay

Traditional corporate strategy centres on establishing defensive strategic positions, building assets and driving synergies from different combinations of assets and/or businesses. Newer models of strategy, however, stress the quality of the strategic process itself, which underpins the ability of the organization to define the 'rules of the game' in its industry rather than simply react to them. This leads to a more organic and dynamic approach to strategy compared with the traditional approach, which is heavily influenced by the machine metaphor.

The demand-driven business model of eBay fundamentally changes the nature of the pricing system and will revolutionize the way companies (particularly retailers) do business. eBay is a true peer-to peer model. It facilitates direct exchanges between people who go to its site to list products for sale or to search listings of products for sale. The actual exchange takes place between individuals. Just as (music file-swapping company) Napster provides a central file directory that allows individuals to swap songs, eBay provides a central listing that allows individuals to buy and sell merchandise. As with Napster, the network members can act as either distributor or consumer.

In essence, eBay makes its money by providing a technology platform that enables users to interact with each other and then skims money off every transaction. This model, like the demand-aggregation models of other e-pioneers, moves from a fixed 'take it or leave it' price determined by sellers (and based most often on cost) to a variable price that actually reflects the true value to the customer as determined by the customers themselves.

Encyclopaedia Britannica

The organization

In 1768, The *Encyclopaedia Britannica* was founded in Edinburgh, Scotland by Colin Macfarquhar, a printer and Andrew Bell, an engraver. Now with its headquarters in Chicago, Illinois, Encyclopaedia Britannica Inc. and Britannica.com Inc. describe themselves as leading providers of learning and knowledge products.

The story

Between 1990 and 1997, hardback sales of the Encyclopaedia Britannica more than halved. During the same period, sales of CD-ROMs blossomed. When Microsoft launched Encarta, it must have seemed like a toy to Britannica's executives. Britannica's intellectual material was far superior to Encarta, whose content was derived from an encyclopaedia traditionally sold at low cost in supermarkets. However, what the Britannica team failed to understand was that parents had bought their encyclopaedia because they wanted to 'do the right thing' for their children. In the 1990s, parents 'did the right thing' by buying a computer. As far as the customer is concerned, Encarta is a near perfect substitute for Britannica.

Add to the equation the enormous cost advantage enjoyed by Encarta which can be produced for around £1 a copy, compared with around £200 to produce a set of Britannica, and the recipe for Britannica's downfall was complete.

Analysis

The arrival of new internet-based firms that are more agile and innovative than the giants are upsetting many a corporate applecart. The internet is helping to put small agile newcomers on a par with large corporations and they are able to compete head on with them for new business. Just as Microsoft could appear from virtually nowhere to usurp the market of mighty IBM, so a few years later Netscape appeared overnight and threatened to undermine the market (and the size) of Microsoft. Who will be next? And where will they come from? In this world, small agile firms have an advantage over giant organizations that are unable to take decisions quickly. This process will accelerate as more and more companies join the e-commerce bandwagon.

The story of Britannica is a demonstration of how quickly the new economics of information have changed the rules of competition. Some might therefore argue that Britannica's woes could be ascribed simply to a set of poor strategic choices.

From a cultural perspective, the deeper question is not simply what mistakes the company made, but rather why those mistakes occurred. The Britannica story is a parable about the dangers of complacency. The fact that a company has been around for over two hundred years doesn't grant it any special rights over its competitors; and yet the company's leaders did seem to assume that they were impervious to external developments.

It took Britannica at least four years to begin to recover its position. These days, the company has set its sights on making full use of all new media, including wireless, to make rich information available to people wherever they need it. The company is also actively syndicating some of its more popular features throughout the internet, making Britannica information more widely accessible.

Seven-Eleven Japan

The organization

Founded in 1973, Seven-Eleven Japan opened its first store in Tokyo the following year. The company established Japan's first true convenience store franchise chain with the stated goal of setting out to 'Modernize and revitalize small and medium-sized retailers', and to achieve 'Mutual prosperity'. According to its website, the company, in partnership with its member stores and customers, 'is committed to continue taking on new and exciting challenges under the motto of "Responding to Change and Strengthening Fundamentals" so that our convenience stores will always be enjoyed by the people we serve'.

As at 31 May 2005, the company had a network of around 28,000 stores in 18 regional districts around the world. Early in 2001, Seven-Eleven lifted the title of biggest retailer in Japan from Daiei, a troubled supermarket giant. Unlike Daiei, and a host of other Japanese companies, Seven-Eleven has defied a sluggish economy to achieve consistent sales growth over the last ten years. In fact, Seven-Eleven has grown sales in every year of its existence. Its pre-tax profits last year were significantly more than those of its nearest rival.

The story

Seven-Eleven has achieved notable success using the internet, with its e-strategy based mainly around proprietary systems. On the whole, it has used the internet to talk to its retail customers, rather than to run its core business. In Japan, it is one of the companies most admired for its effective use of electronic communications.

By the mid-1980s Seven-Eleven Japan had already replaced old-fashioned cash registers with electronic point-of-sale systems that monitored customer purchases. By 1992, it had overhauled its information technology systems four times.

In 1995, before the internet wave had reached Japan to any degree, the company went for a new system based around proprietary –barely tested let alone proven – technology.

It worked, and it gave Seven-Eleven four big advantages.

1. The first was in its ability to track customer needs at a time when deregulation was making shoppers more picky. According to Makoto Usui, who heads the information systems department at Seven-Eleven: "We believed that the nature of competition was changing. Instead of pushing products on to customers, companies were being pulled by customer needs. In this environment, the battleground was at the stores themselves – the interface between businesses and customers."
2. The company collects sales information from every store three times a day, and analyzes it in roughly 20 minutes. As a result, it has bang-up-to-date information about which goods or packaging appeal to customers.
3. The technology helps Seven-Eleven to predict daily trends, particularly important as customers become more fickle, and product cycles are shortening. It does this partly by monitoring the weather, a critical factor in predicting food purchases.
4. The company's technology has vastly improved the efficiency of its supply chain. Orders flow quickly.

Analysis

Much of Seven-Eleven's success can obviously be attributed to its highly effective use. It pioneered many techniques for using the internet that remain state of the art to this day.

Another reason is the company's generally cautious management. While rivals expanded, in retrospect, recklessly over the past decade and then had to announce the closure of hundreds of stores, Seven-Eleven took the view that it would stop opening new stores if sales at existing ones declined sharply. As a result, Seven-Eleven's finances are extremely healthy and largely debt-free.

Vermeer Technologies

The organization

Founded in April 1994 by Dr Charles H. Ferguson and Randy Forgaard, Vermeer Technologies Inc. pioneered the development of powerful, easy-to-use world wide web authoring tools that allow end users and professionals to publish on the web without programming. The company's first product, FrontPage, enabled virtually any company to quickly and easily gain the business benefits of web publishing.

The story

REDMOND, Wash. – January 16, 1996 – Microsoft Corp. today announced the acquisition of Vermeer Technologies Inc., a pioneer of visual, standards-based web publishing tools based in Cambridge, Mass. Vermeer's flagship software application, FrontPage™, is a critically acclaimed tool for easily creating and managing rich web documents without programming. FrontPage will become a key component of Microsoft's strategy to provide a full range of tools that put the power of web publishing, for both the internet and intranets, in the hands of the broadest range of computer users.

"Millions of productivity-applications users want an easier way to participate in the excitement and enhanced productivity of the web," said Bill Gates, Chairman and CEO of Microsoft. "Vermeer's FrontPage fills the wide gap between simple HTML page editors and high-end, professional Web publishing systems available today."

"Access to Microsoft's resources and channel partnerships will allow us to realize our vision of 'Webtop publishing' on a broader scale," said John Mandile, Vermeer's President and Chief Executive Officer. Vermeer coined the phrase 'webtop publishing' to define the process of creating websites using its innovative visual tools.

Microsoft press release

In 1994, Charles Ferguson – consultant, writer and holder of a PhD from the Massachusetts Institute of Technology – set up a company called Vermeer Technologies, named after his favourite painter. It was not the easiest of times to launch a start-up in Silicon Valley, with the US emerging gingerly from a recession, a flat stock market, and the internet yet to be taken seriously by those with money to invest. Yet within two years he sold the company to Microsoft for $133 million, in the process making a fortune for himself and his associates.

Vermeer's 'very cool, very big idea' was FrontPage, the first software product for creating and managing a website, which is now bundled with Microsoft Office and boasts several million users worldwide.

Ferguson tells the story of Vermeer in his book *High Stakes, No Prisoners*. Cue another self-congratulatory business book about how somebody made their millions on the market? Actually no. Ferguson gives a 'warts and all' view into the inner workings of Silicon Valley. In one of his most memorable lines, he describes it as a place where 'one finds little evidence that the meek shall inherit the earth'.

Ferguson is unerringly candid throughout the book, naming names of the people he came across – many of them big movers and the shakers in the industry – and saying what he really thinks of them. Ferguson is very tough on himself, too, owning up to the mistakes his start-up made, and detailing his own shortcomings as a person and a businessman. There can't be many business books around where the index lists, under the heading of the author's name, 'mistakes of', 'naïveté of', and 'paranoia of'.

This is how Ferguson describes a ten-week period beginning in early September 1995, when Vermeer Technologies went from being an unknown development-phase company to being the hottest, coolest start-up in the United States:

> *September through Christmas 1995 would prove to be the most exciting yet punishing months of my professional life.*
>
> *One year earlier, we'd had to fight for months to raise $4 million. Even in March, when we had tried to counter NaviSoft's product launch, nobody had paid us the slightest attention. But by the end*

of September, we had the opposite problem, and it was a very serious problem indeed. Everyone either wanted a piece of our hide or they wanted us dead because we threatened them. And my problems were by no means confined to the outside world. To the contrary, I needed to defend both Vermeer and myself against our investors and our newly hired CEO just as much as against external threats. Events were moving at the speed of light, everything was connected to everything else, and there was essentially nobody I could talk to about it. So these developments brought astonishing highs and great personal fulfillment, but also brutal fights, extreme stress, and painful lessons.

Even through August, we had been quite secretive. While we had been speaking to potential partners, large customers, and analysts, we did so very selectively, under nondisclosure, and usually without revealing sensitive technology or strategic plans. But by September our product was nearly done, and it was time to announce ourselves to the world. Our timing was perfect: as we had planned, we could launch in the peak of the fall season. We wanted business, and there was no further point in concealing what either we or our product did. Furthermore, it was also time to raise more money. So it was time to show our stuff. When we did, the response was, as they say, overwhelming.

So when Peter Amstein and I arrived at the room we'd been assigned for our presentation at Dick Shaffer's Digital Media Outlook conference on September 11, 1995, we found the place packed and the atmosphere electric.Every seat and every square inch was occupied. Venture capitalists, investment bankers, technology executives and industry gurus were lined up along the walls, with more straining to hear from the doorway and the corridor outside. Everyone had already heard of us, but none of them had ever seen our presentations or software before. They liked what they saw. Afterward we were surrounded by people shoving cards at us, wanting meetings, asking if we were raising money, inviting us to conferences, offering partnerships.

Analysis

The Vermeer start-up and sale is an example of strategy in the fast lane. Remember that Charles Ferguson launched Vermeer Technologies from his original idea in late 1993, started shipping FrontPage 1.0 in October 1995, and had sold the company by Christmas of that year. Ferguson himself describes start-ups as 'the intellectual equivalent of driving a small, fast convertible with the top down, the stereo playing Keith Jarrett, Bach, or J.J. Cale very loud, doing a hundred miles an hour on an empty road at sunset'.

Strategy isn't always about carefully considered actions and well thought through plans. For Ferguson, the experience was visceral, immediate and intense.

In terms of the strategic lessons that can be drawn from this example, we need to start by acknowledging that Ferguson achieved something pretty rare. For most of us, the chance of being acquired for massive dollars is about the same as your chance of winning the lottery. It could happen, but only a fool banks on it.

There are other, broader lessons. In general, companies that focus on acquisition put themselves in a dangerous position by closing off their options. Also, there are relatively few potential suitors for most companies, and each may pass over a start-up for a variety of reasons – issues involving geography, personalities or technical integration for example. Finally, it's worth remembering that a buy out is driven by fundamentals like the quality of a company's management team, execution, technology, and strategy. Imitating what another company has done is generally a poor path to take.

Perhaps what the Vermeer story demonstrates above all is that the New Economy is actually the entrepreneurial economy. As the pace of change in global markets and technology has accelerated, entrepreneurs have seized the opportunities created by that change. This can be a hugely profitable exercise, but the business highway is littered with the burnt-out wrecks of failed ventures.

Sources and further reading

Charles H Ferguson, *High Stakes, No Prisoners: A – Winner's Tale of Greed and Glory in the Internet Wars*, Times Business, 1999

Best practice: pulling it all together

So what can we conclude from the case studies in this section? Here are five key themes that run through the examples we have looked at:

Companies mirror their founders

Edgar Schein has described how organizations start with founders and entrepreneurs whose personal assumptions and values gradually create a certain way of thinking and operating, and if their companies are successful, those ways of thinking and operating come to be taken for granted as the 'right' way to run a business. Michael Dell's personal stamp is all over his company. In a similar way, Seven-Eleven's values and culture were evident from its very early days.

It is crisis not comfort that propels significant change

When all is going well for a business, changing the formula is often the last thing on anybody's mind. Encyclopaedia Britannica needed to be shaken up by a competitor before it could accept the reality that longevity is no guarantor of survival.

Achieving business success requires a sense of purpose first and good management practices second

An organization is not a club – its purpose is not solely to look after the well-being of its members. Similarly, Charles Ferguson's sale of Vermeer Technologies was an intoxicating experience first and a rational process second.

Different strokes for different folks

Organizations achieve success in very different ways and by focusing on what is most important to them. For Dell, the focus was on culture.

In some cases, the need is to focus on dangers within the organization. For Encyclopaedia Britannica, the enemy was mindset.

There is no such thing as the ideal set of organizational behaviours or management practices, except in relation to what the organization is trying to do. A team of fire fighters will necessarily have a different set of operating patterns to an advertising agency. Even though our personality and preferences might make us better suited to work in some places rather than others, this doesn't make one environment automatically 'better' than another.

On a similar tack, different people look for different things out of their careers. Some people look mainly for a sense of security and stability, while others seek out roles with a high level of challenge. Some want to manage people and resources; others prefer to pursue roles requiring a high level of technical competence.

Let's do this thing

Successful companies are those that came up with a way forward that is timely, credible, simple and – most crucial of all – which is able to be readily applied. In the final analysis, organizational success comes down to implementation. The best ideas poorly executed are worthless.

SIX
Annotated bibliography

This section is a guided tour to around 50 or so key books written about various aspects of e-business.

Mastering the Digital Market Place: Practical Strategies for Competitiveness in the E-business

Douglas F. Aldrich • John Wiley, 2000

In the digital economy, argues Aldrich, there are two key measures of value: time (as in how much time your product or service will save the customer) and content (information, knowledge, or services that provide added value to the customer). He goes on to outline a new business model which he calls the Digital Value Network (DVN), a community of electronically linked business partners that work together to produce value for the customer as the customer defines it, and offers strategies for creating and sustaining it. An intriguing business model, and Aldrich makes a compelling case for it becoming a blueprint for success in the digital revolution.

The Last Days of the Giants?

Robert Baldock • John Wiley, 2000

Robert Baldock sees major problems ahead for any of us working in those organizations that have come to believe that their sheer size will protect them from the unpredictability of the next few years. 'The environment in which the culture of 'bigness' blossomed is fast disappearing in many industries,' he tells us. However, the question mark in the title of Baldock's book is significant – the corporate giants of late 20th century may be in serious trouble but he believes they can survive in the intensely competitive environment of the 21st if they radically alter the way they do things. The optimal 21st century organization, says Baldock, will be a buyer-driven virtual enterprise that satisfies consumer intentions.

The Age of E-tail: Conquering the New World of Electronic Shopping

Alex Birch, Philipp Gerbert, & Dirk Schneider • Capstone, 2000

In *The Age of E-tail*, the authors explore 12 key themes that are relevant to any business that is considering going down the e-commerce route. As well as exploring these themes in depth, the book contains some nice touches. Each chapter contains a 'searchlight' summary of key points as well as a list of websites for the companies highlighted by the authors as examples of good and bad practice. Throughout the book, there are useful tips and wrinkles for the e-tail novice. More crucially, the authors set out a coherent and credible approach to e-tail which speaks as much to the long established bricks and mortar business as it does to the fresh-faced start-up proposition. As a guide to how to enter successfully the world of electronic shopping, it hasn't yet been bettered.

The Meme Machine

Susan Blackmore • Oxford University Press, 1999

Once humans learned to receive, copy and retransmit memes – in essence a captivating idea, behaviour, or skill that can be transferred from one person to another by imitation – the rest, says Blackmore, is a foregone conclusion. Memetic competition shapes our minds and culture, just as natural selection has shaped our physical evolution. But why should this matter to us and the organizations we work for? Well for a start, it explains why the sexual adventures of an errant senior manager would grip the corporate imagination more than the latest set of financial figures. Blackmore explores her subject with great panache. Some readers who like to explore both sides of an argument before making up their own minds may find her sure-footed advocacy a little overpowering, but for the rest of us *The Meme Machine* is a riveting and provocative read.

The Electronic B@zaar

Robin Bloor • Nicholas Brealey, 2000

Bloor's mix of leading-edge IT analysis, historical perspective and a sound grasp of economic principles makes for an informative and entertaining account of the new economic landscape. The Electronic B@zaar occasionally reads as though it has been put through some kind of Tom Peters-style writer software, but nonetheless the book is a compelling call-to-arms for anybody seeking practical tips about making the transition from bricks-and-mortar to successful e-business.

Knowledge Capitalism

Alan Burton-Jones • Oxford University Press, 1999

Burton-Jones marshals an impressive range of evidence in this closely argued exploration of how the shift to a knowledge-based economy is redefining the shape and nature of organizations. He also describes the emergence of a new breed of capitalist, one dependent on knowledge rather than physical resources. There are plenty of easier reads about the knowledge economy on the market, but those looking for substance rather than eye-catching glibness will be pleased to find in *Knowledge Capitalism* a book that provides frequent moments of insight without compromising gravitas.

E-business and E-commerce Management

Dave Chaffey • FT Prentice Hall, 2003

The second edition of *E-Business and E-Commerce Management* builds on the excellent coverage and balanced approach of the first edition.

Drawing on perspectives and models from disciplines as diverse as information systems, strategy, marketing, operations and human resources management. This new edition also features increased coverage of legal and regulatory issues, not-for-profit organizations and a wider range of international case studies.

A comprehensive assessment of the management issues faced in implementing e-business solutions, this book is suitable for students or practitioners of e-business, e-commerce or e-marketing at any level. Each chapter contains management issues, activities and answers, case studies, questions for debate, self-assessment exercises, discussion, essay and exam questions, further reading, web links and more.

Built to Last

James Collins and Jerry Porras • HarperBusiness, 1994

When *Built to Last* appeared in 1994, it was the product of a six year investigation by James Collins and Jerry Porras, both Stanford professors at the time, which set out to uncover the underlying principles that could yield enduring, great companies. For the book, they examined 18 companies that had significantly outperformed the general stock market over a number of decades. The companies looked at included Disney, General Electric, Hewlett-Packard, IBM and Wal-Mart. So what's this got to do with e-business? Well, implicit on every page of *Built to Last* is a simple question – why would a company settle for creating something mediocre that does little more than make money, when it could create something outstanding that makes a lasting contribution as well? At a time when it seems the lifespan of some dot.com companies can be measured in weeks or months rather than decades, this question strikes at the heart of business and life in the New Economy. Let's hope that founders of New Economy businesses come to realize that it is better to concentrate primarily on building an organization rather than on hitting a market just right with a visionary product idea and riding the growth curve of an attractive product cycle. Let's also hope that the primary output of their efforts is the tangible implementation of a great and sustainable idea and that their greatest creation is the company itself and what it stands for.

The Weightless World

Diane Coyle • Capstone, 1997

In *The Weightless World,* Diane Coyle, who is economics editor at *The Independent,* maps out the economic and social landscape in a world increasingly transformed by the digital revolution, not to mention globalism and the disappearance of many of the old securities. For Coyle, weightlessness is a 'symbol of the economic effects of the clusters of advances in information and communication technology,' and the financial markets 'the ultimate embodiment of weightlessness, or in other words the intangibility of an increasing proportion of modern economies'. What gives the concept particular potency is the manner in which technological change interacts with other fundamental changes like demographic and social trends and the grand sweep of social history, creating, in Coyle's word's, 'the age of insecurity'.

Blur

Stan Davis and Christopher Meyer • Addison-Wesley, 1998

The authors, who are both based at the Ernst & Young Center for Business Innovation in Boston, maintain that 'connectivity, speed, and the growth of intangible value' have catapulted business into a period of unprecedented transition that demands immediate and creative attention. These three elements in combination, say Davis and Meyer, 'are blurring the rules and redefining our businesses and our lives. They are destroying solutions, such as mass production, segmented pricing, and standardized jobs, that worked for the relatively slow, unconnected industrial world'.

Future Wealth

Stan Davis and Christopher Meyer
Harvard Business School Press, 2000

In *Future Wealth* – described as the companion volume to Potted Biographys' best-selling book *Blur* – Davis and Meyer identify three major consequences of the newly connected economy: risk as opportunity, not only as threat; the growing efficiency of financial markets for human capital; and the need for new forms of social capital. They go on to explain why they think we are headed toward a new stage of economic development in which 'human and intellectual capital [is] the most highly valued resource'.

In the Company of Giants

Rama Dev Jager & Rafael Ortiz • McGraw-Hill, 1997

Described by Potted Biographys as a set of 'candid conversations with the visionaries of the digital world,' the book comprises transcripts of 15 interviews, each one preceded by a brief pen picture of the interviewee. Those featured include Bill Gates, Andy Grove, Bill Hewlett and Michael Dell, and so the book does live up to its title. Although there are some useful tidbits and quotable responses to questions, the book also serves to demonstrate how much things have changed in the years since *In the Company of Giants* was published.

Post-Capitalistic Society

Peter Drucker • HarperCollins, 1993

An early picture of e-business which has held up extremely well over the intervening years. Tom Peters may be the most famous living management guru, but Drucker is probably the most respected and insightful.

StrikingitRich.com

Jaclyn Easton • McGraw-Hill, 1999

Sub-titled *profiles of 23 incredibly successful companies you've probably never heard of,* Jaclyn Easton's rigorously researched and extremely readable book proves that websites don't have to be high profile extravaganzas to make serious money. The sites demonstrate that it is perfectly possible for a website to achieve a profit quickly if an idea is well conceived and executed and if start-up costs are managed tightly.

Entrepreneurship and the Wired Life: Work in the Wake of Careers

Fernando Flores & John Gray • Demos, 2000

The career, as an institution, is in unavoidable decline according to this fascinating pamphlet from independent UK think-tank Demos. The authors describe two work patterns – the Wired and the Entrepreneurial – which might replace the traditional career work pattern. In a nutshell, the Wired life/work pattern replaces the lifelong identity of the career with a series of 'brief habits', at the heart of which is spontaneity rather than continuity of projects and relationships. With the Entrepreneurial life/work pattern, Flores and Gray widen out the narrow economic definition of entrepreneurship to include all manner of activities which initiate meaningful change in a context of shared responsibility. This could be in commerce, service or in society in general. The authors go on to examine these new forms of working life in some detail and consider the implications for individuals and communities. They conclude that core institutions – from education to pensions – need restructuring to support these changes. At only 48 pages long, *Entrepreneurship and the Wired Life* is that rare phenomenon – a business book that could usefully have been double the length.

The Tipping Point: How Little Things Can Make a Big Difference

Malcolm Gladwell • Little Brown, 2000

Why do some minority tastes remain strictly minority, while others extend into the mainstream? *The Tipping Point* is a well written and racy exploration of what lies behind the point when a small fad acquires critical mass and takes off. It's very readable but the central idea isn't really enough to sustain a whole book – no surprise then to discover that it began its life as a long article in New Yorker magazine.

Net Gain

John Hagel III & Arthur G. Armstrong
Harvard Business School Press, 1997

Well-written and insightful view of the e-business focusing on how virtual communities can expand markets. Highly recommended by Kevin Kelly in his bibliography at the back of *New Rules for the New* Economy.

Online Consumer Psychology: Understanding and Influencing Consumer Behavior in the Virtual World

Curtis P Haugtvedt et al. • Lawrence Erlbaum Associates, Inc, 2005

Online Consumer Psychology addresses many of the issues created by the internet and goes beyond the topic of advertising and the web to include topics such as customization, site design, word of mouth processes, and the study of consumer decision making while online. The theories and research methods help provide greater insight into the processes underlying consumer behavior in online environments. Broken into six sections, this book focuses on the advantages of the internet's ability to bring like-minded individuals from around the room into one forum; examines issues related to advertising, specifically click-through rates and advertising content placed within gaming online and wireless networks; provides readers with reasons why consumers customize products and the benefits of customization; discusses the psychological effects of site design; asks the question of whether the internet empowers consumers to make better decisions; and discusses research tools that can be used online.

The Elephant and the Flea

Charles Handy • Hutchinson, 2001

In this book, self-styled social philosopher Handy explores the business world of the 21st century which he claims 'will be a world of fleas and elephants, of large conglomerates and small individual entities, of large political and economic blocs and small countries'. The smart thing, it seems, is to be the flea on the back of the elephant because a flea can be global as easily as one of the elephants but can more easily be swept away. Elephants are a guarantee of continuity but fleas provide the innovation. A fascinating premise, outlined lucidly by Handy.

The New Century

Eric Hobsbawm • Little Brown, 2000

In which the late pre-eminent historian (you won't find a better account of the twentieth century than his *Age of Extremes*) offers his analysis of the current state of the world. Although the scope of this book goes much wider than the e-business, there's one chapter in particular – entitled *The Global Village* – that offers a lucid, cool-headed, and reasoned assessment of the global economy. It's a much needed antidote to the starry-eyed hyperbole that seems to dominate the globalization debate.

On the Edge

Will Hutton and Anthony Giddens • Jonathan Cape, 2000

On the Edge draws together ten original contributions by leading thinkers like Paul Volcker, Manuel Castells, Arlie Russell Hochschild and George Soros. The overall conclusion seems to be that global capitalism does have huge potential for good but is just as likely to create a set of consequences that most of us would rather avoid. Co-author and Industrial Society boss Will Hutton describes global capitalism as 'precarious and potentially dangerous'. An important book that takes a clear-eyed view of its subject.

Starting and Running a Business on the Internet

Tim Ireland • Take That Ltd, 2000

Coming in at just 109 pages and at a quarter of the cost of similar books, *Starting and Running a Business on the Internet* is an admirably concise and accessible guide for those wanting to know the practical steps involved in setting up a successful internet business, from first conception through to promoting the site. A cautionary note, though.

Ireland's particular strength rests in his knowledge of the mechanics of setting up a new internet business – from acquiring a domain name, through to 'going live' and taking orders from around the world. He does not set out to provide a comprehensive guide to the overall business start-up process and so readers will find nothing on raising capital, hiring staff, business planning *et al*. These reservations aside, this book is a useful *vade mecum* for the would-be internet entrepreneur.

Simplicity

Bill Jensen • HarperCollins, 2000

One of the few books written from the knowledge worker's perspective. Jam-packed with tools and techniques for the individual, it also contains some useful insights on to how to build corporate infrastructures so the company is the tool of the worker, not the other way around. Also worth checking out www.simplerwork.com, the companion website.

Wired Life

Charles Jonscher • Anchor, 1999

Lord Reith's goal for the BBC was that it should inform, educate and entertain. Harvard academic and successful businessman Jonscher achieves this mix brilliantly in *Wired Life*. Neither Luddite nor technophile in outlook, Jonscher takes a clear-eyed look at the digital age and argues convincingly that the human spirit must be master of, and not slave to, the new information technologies.

Competitive Intelligence

Larry Kahaner • Simon and Schuster, 1996

In a world of rapid technological change where new and sometimes surprising competitors can suddenly appear, a company's success will increasingly depend on how effectively it can gather, analyze and use information. According to Kahaner, companies that can turn raw information into powerful intelligence will build market share, launch new products, increase profits and destroy competitors. Using a series of case studies, this book provides a useful overview of a number of intelligence gathering techniques, even if some of them – benchmarking, for example, are pretty familiar by now. An informative book, nonetheless, that illustrates how much information is either a matter of public record or is readily and legally accessible.

The One Best Way

Robert Kanigel • Little Brown, 1997

The One Best Way is an illuminating biography of Frederick W. Taylor, the efficiency expert and 'the father of scientific management'. Although he lived through little of it – he died in 1915, aged 59 – Taylor's influence on the 20th century is unquestionable. Peter Drucker, for example, rates him alongside Freud and Darwin as a maker of the modern world. And, despite its critics, Taylorism lives on, whether in the form of reengineering (a direct descendant of scientific management), the continuing debate about the de-skilling of jobs, or the global standardization of companies like McDonald's. At 570 pages, the book is definitely top-heavy with detail. However, as an introduction to arguably the world's first management consultant, it makes fascinating reading.

The Complexity Advantage

Susanne Kelly and Mary Ann Allison • McGraw Hill, 1999

This book argues that anybody operating in a business world growing ever more complex would benefit from an understanding of complexity theory. *The complexity advantage* represents a serious and sustained attempt to incorporate complexity principles and methodologies into business thinking. The more general reader may initially be baffled by some of the terminology but persistence will pay off.

Out of Control: the new biology of machines

Kevin Kelly • Addison Wesley Inc, 1994

Out of Control is a sprawling, provocative and massive (at over 600 pages) exploration of the organic nature of human-made systems. It's crammed with original insights all clustered around Kelly's view that our technological future is headed toward a neo-biological civilization. There are those who would argue that this is Kelly's true masterpiece.

Community Building on the Web

Amy Jo Kim • Peachpit Press, 2000

A thriving website, according to Kim, is one that engages people and makes them want to return time and time again. Those that encourage the participation of visitors go beyond simply offering a source of information and provide a platform for visitors, or community members, to meet and exchange thoughts and ideas. Kim's practical knowledge of building online communities comes over strongly, her tips and advice convincing and her enthusiasm infectious. The book has a companion website which can be found at www.naima.com/community

The Age of Heretics

Art Kleiner • Nicholas Brealey Publishing, 1996

'Corporate heretics' are those people within an organization who believe in a truth that contradicts the conventional wisdom of their time. Many of them see their ideas ignored or their efforts undermined. Nonetheless, their ideas eventually take root. Kleiner describes the impact on the history of post-war business of a succession of these maverick, independent-thinking individuals. He goes on to show how the heretical ideas of the 1950s, '60s and '70s – self-managed teams, customer focus, scenario planning and so on – have now been absorbed into mainstream corporate thinking. Perhaps his conclusion is overly upbeat. Are today's organizations really 'beginning to understand how much there is to learn from dissent?' Is life really that much easier for heretics currently working for organizations who believe themselves to be infallible?

Living on Thin Air

Charles Leadbeater • Viking, 1999

In *Living on Thin Air*, Leadbeater argues that society will need to be organized around the creation of knowledge capital and social capital, rather than simply being dominated by the power of financial capital. He draws on research in California, Japan, Germany and the Far East to show how his provocative manifesto might be achieved. He puts over his ideas in a highly informative and accessible way and argues his case well, although some readers may feel that his take on the future is a little more optimistic than the facts seem to justify.

The Cluetrain Manifesto

Rick Levine, Christopher Locke, Doc Searls and David Weinberger
Perseus Publishing, 2000

The story of *The Cluetrain Manifesto* goes like this: it began in the early part of 1999 when the book's authors – four respected insiders from the technology sector – decided to use a website as a forum for articulating what they described as 'a set of principles we believe will determine the future experience of both individuals and organizations Online'. The principles are a mixture of declarations that business is fundamentally a human enterprise, and devastating swipes at a business establishment seemingly intent on viewing the internet as a market place to colonize rather than a community to join. The authors compiled their manifesto, published it on a website and invited visitors to the site to sign up to it. Word about the site spread virally through corporate America, and the site rapidly attained a cult status. The book, published in 2000, gave the authors the opportunity to expand and augment the contents of the manifesto. They do this through seven chapters filled with their stories and observations about how business gets done and how the internet will change it all.

Understanding Media

Marshall McLuhan • Sphere, 1964

Marshall McLuhan's investigation into the state of the then emerging mass media is an exuberant, provocative, and scatter-gun piece of work. Much of the challenge he made to 60s' sensibilities and assumptions about how and what we communicate still holds good.

Understanding Media reads like a work in progress that connects to the e-business in the same way that H. G. Wells linked to the Apollo moon landings.

The Death of Competition

James F. Moore • HarperCollins, 1996

Business as ecosystem – Moore explores the biological metaphor in great detail and with considerable insight. One of the first and arguably the best exploration of leadership and strategy in a future that Moore envisions will be characterized by organized chaos.

World Class: Thriving Locally in the Global Economy

Rosabeth Moss Kanter • Simon and Schuster, 1995

Professor Moss Kanter tackles big issues in this book: globalization, the future of capitalism, communitarianism, xenophobia and cultural imperialism. It is a disquieting book – her world is one in which the new colonialism will be brought about by a techno-elite. When she does stop to consider the human side to all this, it is to conclude that sensible xenophobics should see the error of their ways and realize that globalization can only do them good. This is an important book because it comes from a woman who has access to very good data indeed, a woman who ought to know. But if her reading of the rise of the new world class is accurate, this is also a very scary book. The global economy promises global dystopia.

Connexity

Geoff Mulgan • Chatto & Windus 1997

Language lovers among us will be heartened to see that Geoff Mulgan, founder and former director of independent think-tank Demos, has revived an old English word to describe a world that is becoming ever more closely and intricately connected. *Connexity* describes the interdependence that stems from our all being tied into a global economy, environment and communication system. For example, by choosing to buy one item of clothes rather than another, we contribute to a process that may ultimately determine whether someone on the other side of the world retains or loses their job; emissions originating in one part of the world can contribute to problems with the ozone layer somewhere else; using the internet or the mobile phone, we can communicate with others at any time and just about anywhere in the world. Mulgan believes that this degree of interconnectedness, where we are all joined together physically, psychologically and informationally, brings a host of opportunities and constraints that carry significant implications for governments, organizations and individuals alike.

Computer Lib

Theodor H. Nelson • Microsoft Press International, 1988

Ted Nelson, part-academic, part-computer visionary, is generally credited with coining the term 'hypertext' and putting it to work as a new mode of publication in the emerging computer technologies of the '60s and '70s. He also conceived a system called Xanadu, recognizably a fore-runner of the world wide web, where electronic documents are linked up. Great book by a true visionary and a true pleasure to read – so why is it out of print? Despite this snub from the publishing world, Nelson retains a loyal following and it is perhaps only natural that the best sources of information about him are internet-based. If you're interested, try www.xanadu.com

The Invisible Continent

Kenichi Ohmae • HarperBusiness, 2000

According to Ohmae, the invisible continent is the world in which businesses now operate, which is like a new, just discovered continent. The invisible continent has dimensions: the Visible Dimension – physical things to buy and make; the Borderless World – inevitable globalization; the Cyber Dimension – the internet, mobile phones; and the Dimension of High Multiples.

Surfing the Edge of Chaos

Richard Pascale, Mark Milleman, Linda Gioja • Texere Publishing, 2000

This book explores how today's business laws have parallels in the laws of nature: evolution creates survivors, genetic mixing breeds stronger descendants, moving too far from core values results in chaos. A bit like Richard Dawkins' *The Selfish Gene*, this book blends scientific information with social comment and history.

The Soul of the Internet

Neil Randall • Thomson Computer Press, 1997

The history of the internet, as told by many of the individuals involved in its development. Randall pulls the story together well, putting the internet's development into its technological, social, educational and commercial contexts. What becomes clear from reading this substantial book is that the developers and builders of the internet outnumber the true visionaries several times over.

The Internet Start-Up Bible

Tess Read, Callum Chace and Simon Rowe • Random House, 2000

The Internet Start-Up Bible is an accessible, well written guide about how to plan, research, fund, market and implement a successful internet-based business model. Potted Biographys take the logical and too often neglected step of applying the same success criteria to dot.com business start-ups as to traditional ventures. Detailed chapters on business planning and attracting venture capital are followed by sections on various aspects of starting up an internet business: technology, design, marketing and launch, before concluding with business growth and flotation. The book is crammed with useful case studies, extensive links and contact addresses and running quotes from business gurus and key books.

Shakedown: How the E-business is Changing Our Lives

Angus Reid • Doubleday Publishing, 1997

As Chairman and CEO of the Angus Reid Group Inc., a leading Canadian polling firm, Angus Reid has been close to the dreams and aspirations of the Canadian people for close to 20 years. In *Shakedown* he describes how three major discontinuities are converging to change the shape of Canadian society for ever. The combination of technological change, globalization and the ageing of the population has meant the end of the 'spend and share era' of national prosperity and optimism that characterized Canada from the '60s to the '80s and the beginning of a new uncertainty era which Reid christens the 'sink or swim' era. The power of this book is in the detail: how these changes are affecting every aspect of Canadian life today and how they will shape the future. Although the book is written for Canadians, its message is universal and is one that we can all readily identify with.

Funky Business

Jonas Ridderstråle and Kjell Nordström • ft.com, 2000

On the face of it, a business book by two Swedish professors about how successful companies differ from their competitors doesn't sound like the most riveting of reads. But *Funky Business* is no dry theoretical tome; and authors Ridderstråle and Nordström are not your standard-issue academics. Unless, that is, it's normal for Swedish business professors to shave their heads, wear leather trousers, describe themselves as funksters, and call their public appearances gigs rather than seminars.

Perhaps it now sounds like you are in for a trip through some familiar corners of the new economy in a light-weight and gimmicky manner redolent of Tom Peters at his worst. Far from it. This book draws extensively from rigorously researched data but presents its findings with wit and intelligence reinforced with excellent examples.

Ridderstråle and Nordström are convinced that we are moving towards a state of super capitalism, with near friction-free markets. As a result, every supplier everywhere has access to the same resources, ideas, methods and technology. The catch is that every consumer now has access to fantastic choice. In such a world, they say that time and talent are the two critical commodities and it is how companies deal with these two factors that determines which companies fall by the wayside and which move through to the next round. The goal, and this is as good as it gets, is to be, as the authors put it, 'momentarily ahead of the game'.

The Clickable Corporation

Jonathan Rosenoer, Douglas Armstrong & J Russell Gates
Free Press, 1999

The Clickable Corporation has a subtitle – *Successful Strategies for Capturing the Internet Advantage* – that makes its intentions very clear. Based on research by three consultants at global consultancy Arthur Andersen, and drawing on evidence from 25 companies including Barnes & Noble, Federal Express, Amazon and Dell, this book sets out to offer an accessible guide aimed at business people who are looking to make optimal and profitable use of the web. Rosenoer, Armstrong and Gates, displaying a level of certainty that seemingly only management consultants can ever muster, tell us that there are eight value propositions that a company must offer through its website – knowledge, choice, convenience, customization, savings, community, entertainment and trust.

Futurize your Enterprise: Business Strategy in the Age of the E-customer

David Siegel • John Wiley, 1999

'Everyone understands that the internet is changing business,' writes Siegel in *Futurize your Enterprise*, 'but most companies still don't understand how to approach the web. They've applied new kinds of marketing and technology, they've put their catalogues online, they put 'com' at the end of their names, and they have little to show for their efforts. That's because the limiting factor online isn't technology, branding, or bandwidth – it's mindset'. According to Siegel, many companies fail to truly understand how e-commerce works, and as a result they fall into some or all of what he calls 'the six common traps of e-commerce'. *Futurize your Enterprise* is really about how companies can avoid these traps and, more positively, become a meaningful player in what Siegel calls the Customer-Led Revolution. He finishes his book by offering some predictions about how the business landscape might develop over the next ten years, as most of the world goes online.

Digital Darwinism

Evan Schwartz • Penguin, 1999

A book title that brings together two of the biggest managerial buzzwords of recent times exerts a certain fascination. According to Schwartz in an interview published on Amazon.com, *Digital Darwinism* is 'a different way of looking at the web economy and how it's co-evolving with the larger business world around it. It's a way of looking at the web as an ecosystem, where the players are scrounging for money and are competing and co-operating with each other as if they were a species in a natural environment'. This is a fascinating premise and one which merits rather more depth than Schwartz brings to the topic. There is a 17-page introduction entitled 'Frenetic Evolution' in which he notes some interesting parallels between Darwin's theory of evolution and the online world. But he goes no further in substantive terms.

There are a few links made to what lies at the heart of *Digital Darwinism,* namely 'seven breakthrough strategies for surviving in the cut-throat web economy,' but occasional allusions to 'survival guides' don't constitute the grand theory that Schwartz seems to promise at the outset. The irony is that the seven strategies themselves are a neat encapsulation of what a business – be it an internet start-up or a bricks-and-mortar offshoot – should be doing to achieve web success.

The Art of the Long View

Peter Schwartz • Doubleday, 1991

When it originally appeared, *The Art of the Long View* was one of the first books to explain and generally demystify the scenario planning techniques developed at Royal/Dutch Shell in the 1970s and 1980s. Peter Schwartz led their scenario planning unit for four years in the early '80s, and so he writes from a background of significant personal experience. In *The Art of the Long View,* he describes how, in practice, scenarios resemble a set of stories, written or spoken, built around carefully constructed plots. 'Scenarios are stories that give meaning to events,' writes Schwartz. They are an old way of organizing knowledge; when used as strategic tools, they confront denial by encouraging – in fact, requiring – the willing suspension of disbelief. Stories can express multiple perspectives on complex events. Creating scenarios, says Schwartz, requires decision-makers to question their broadest assumptions about the way the world works. Good scenarios are plausible, surprising, and have the power to break old stereotypes. Using scenarios is 'rehearsing the future' such that, by recognizing the warning signs, an organization can adapt, and act effectively. As Schwartz puts it, 'Decisions which have been pre-tested against a range of what fate may offer are more likely to stand the test of time, produce robust and resilient strategies, and create distinct competitive advantage. Ultimately, the result of scenario planning is not a more accurate picture of tomorrow but better thinking and an ongoing strategic conversation about the future'.

The Social Life of Information

John Seely Brown and Paul Duguid
Harvard Business School Press, 2000

Potted Biographys put forward a convincing and eloquent argument that human sociability needs to play an important role in the digital world. They explore the importance of placing information in a social context, highlighting the dangers inherent in separating, in their words, 'text from context'. Their conclusion that the digital world stills needs a human heart at its centre is both plausible and uplifting.

Customers.com

Patricia Seybold • Random House, 1998

Customers.com offers practical and implementable advice based on the sound premise that any e-commerce initiative has to begin with the customer. The book contains some instructive case studies about how companies like Hertz, PhotoDisc, National Semiconductor and Wells Fargo are using the internet successfully. Shelfloads of books have now been written on this theme but what sets *Customers.com* apart is Seybold's talent for communicating her 20 years of experience in the technology industry in an accessible and no-nonsense writing style.

Profit Patterns

Slywotzky, Morrison, Moser, Mundt and Quella • John Wiley, 1999

A total re-questioning of different types of profit models is a necessary aspect of success in the e-business. In *Profit Patterns,* Potted Biographys introduce pattern thinking as a means of enabling managers to envision opportunities and design winning strategies ahead of the competition. 'Like the best chess players,' they write, 'masters of business pattern recognition, instead of seeing chaos, know how to identify the strategic picture unfolding within the complexity and discover the pattern behind it all'. The book describes a set of 30 patterns that have occurred in industry after industry, shifting billions of pounds in market value from those who 'missed' them to those who 'mastered' them. Company case studies that feature in the book include Dell, Microsoft and Amazon. Not an easy read particularly, but one that rewards attention.

The Wealth of Knowledge

Thomas A Stewart • Nicholas Brealey, London, 2001

Stewart follows up his best-selling *Intellectual Capital* by looking at how to apply the concept to managing knowledge assets and thereby gaining competitive edge. A knowledge economy 'bible' in the making.

Search Me: The Surprising Success of Google

Neil Taylor • Cyan Books, 2005

A fascinating history of Google.com from its humble beginnings in the garage of two former Stanford University students to its development into the search engine of choice for internet users worldwide.

Future Shock

Alvin Toffler • Bantam, 1970

More than three decades ago, Toffler anticipated the waves of anxiety that the technological revolution would engender in this groundbreaking exploration of what happens to people and society when overwhelmed by change.

The E-Code: 33 Internet Superstars Reveal 43 Ways to Make Money Online Almost Instantly Using Only E-Mail!

Joe Vitale & Jo Han Mock • John Wiley, 2005

In this book, the authors present what they call a proven collection of simple and effective ways to make money online. The *E-Code* reveals 47 simple ideas by 32 internet superstars that anyone can use to make money on the Internet right now and with only e-mail. Each short, succinct chapter by an internet celebrity presents one strategy for profiting and offers step-by-step guidance on implementing it to for greatest profit effect.

The Entertainment Economy: the mega-media forces that are shaping our lives

Michael J Wolf • Random House, 1999

In *The Entertainment Economy*, Michael Wolf argues that media and entertainment have moved beyond mere culture to become the driving force of the global retail economy. As he puts it, 'There's no business without show business'. In this world where 'entertainment content has become a key differentiator in virtually every aspect of the broader consumer economy', all consumer businesses need to acknowledge the multi-level relationships that entertainment businesses set out to build with their customers. In other words, in a world where businesses compete primarily for the time and attention of customers, content becomes king, and the quality of the experience the clincher.

This book is a compelling read for anyone who is even remotely interested in the media and entertainment world. Its great strength is that Michael Wolf is real industry insider who continually engages the reader with examples and stories from across the industry. However, the danger is that the book's conversational style and entertainment-centric focus might mislead people into viewing it as an enjoyable and insightful read rather than a groundbreaking work with the potential to speak to a wider audience. *The Entertainment Economy* has some valid and highly relevant messages for the business world, but the book's lack of charts, tables, graphs, or even any bulletpoints means that extracting these messages requires quite a bit of work on the business reader's part.

Twilight of Sovereignty

Walt Wriston • Charles Scribner & Sons, 1992

Walt Wriston, former chairman of Citicorp, addresses the issues facing the corporations of America and the world during the 1990s and beyond. He argues that centralized corporate/political power has disappeared; that the world has been transformed by technology; and that negotiation will rule the world in future. Well worth a read (if you can track down a copy).

SEVEN
Tracking e-business trends

For readers wanting to keep up to date with e-business developments, this chapter recommends publications and websites that are worth dipping into from time to time:

BBC news online

Good coverage of mainstream technology-related issues
www.news.bbc.co.uk/1/hi/technology/default.stm

CIO Magazine: The E-Business Research Center

Examines the current state and future directions of conducting commerce on the internet through articles, events, discussion groups and informational links.
www.cio.com

eCommerce Web Center

Good all round US e-commerce site full of good marketing tips plus some worthwhile links.
www.ecominfocenter.com

Economist

The best single source of information about what is happening in the world. A mainstream publication but one that will take on some big topics from time to time, and one whose take on the e-business is variably insightful and clear-eyed.
www.economist.com

Fast Company

A US-published monthly magazine that has been an essential read since it started up in 1996. Of late, though, the content – while still excellent – has been swamped by increasing volumes of advertising. The companion website is just about the best free site around on e-business and the future world of work (it also carries material not found in the magazine).
www.fastcompany.com/home.html

Financial Times

Of all the UK dailies, *The Financial Times* provides the best in-depth coverage of IT and work-related issues. Well worth keeping an eye out for their occasional information technology surveys.
www.ft.com

Fucked Company

An irreverent spoof of *Fast Company* that, like the very best Dilbert-cartoons, uses humor as a vehicle for revealing some painful truths about working in the e-business.
www.fuckedcompany.com

Gilder Technology Report

Anybody interested in the present and future impact of technology on the US and world economy will find Gilder's articles an intriguing set of appetizers from this seminal thinker and iconoclast. Not always easy to understand but worth making the effort.
www.gildertech.com/index.asp

Harvard Business Review

Still the most authoritative business bi-monthly on the block. It has tended in the past to be more mainstream than truly groundbreaking in its coverage of business issues. That said, HBR has responded

well to the challenge to traditional business thinking posed by the e-business, and recent issues have generally contained two or three relevant articles. Also, if you are interested in getting the lowdown on forthcoming books from Harvard's publishing wing several months before publication, the magazine consistently trails major books with articles from the authors in question. The website provides an overview of the contents of the magazine – very limited free content these days but the executive summaries are there and they are often all you need.
www.hbsp.harvard.edu/home.html

(The) Information Economy

This website is overseen by economist Hal Varian, co-author of *Information Rules*, and lists hundreds of papers, works in progress and links to other information economy websites. An almost overwhelming resource but one that hasn't been bettered for thoroughness.
www.sims.berkeley.edu/resources/infoecon/

New Media Knowledge

A publicly funded body based at the University of Westminster which analyzes and facilitates the growth of the UK's digital media industries.
www.nmk.co.uk/

New Scientist

Important science and technology stories will often appear here first. New Scientist also gives good coverage to emerging thinking in the scientific community.
www.newscientist.com

New Thinking

New Thinking is a weekly, approximately 500-word exploration of the digital age, produced by Gerry McGovern, former CEO of Nua and author of *The Caring Economy*. Taking a broad, philosophical view of things, it is written in clear, concise language and delivers some

useful comments and ideas. It is available by email and is free. To subscribe, go to McGovern's website.
www.gerrymcgovern.com

New York Times

Good source of articles on the latest e-business developments in the US. Worth subscribing to their daily news e-mail. Full articles can be accessed at no cost for a day or two; once 'archived', there's a charge.
www.nytimes.com

Sloan Management Review

The management journal of the Massachusetts Institute of Technology (MIT). Published quarterly, it features articles by some of the world's leading strategic thinkers, and has a genuinely global range.
www.sloanreview.mit.edu/smr/

Time

Weekly news magazine that gives good, positive coverage to e-business issues and people. That said, *Time* is a mainstream publication and so is unlikely to be absolutely at the forefront of e-business thinking. Nonetheless, in recent months it has carried special features on e-commerce, the future of work, and so on.
www.time.com/europe

The Utne Reader

A digest, whose editors scan thousands of small and alternative magazines. Not that well focused perhaps, but worth visiting for occasional gems.
www.utne.com

Wired

Monthly American magazine that is good at picking up e-business trends about six months before they become trends.
www.wired.com/wired/

World Future Society

Not-for-profit educational and scientific organization that explores how social and technological developments are shaping the future.
www.wfs.org

EIGHT
An e-business glossary

An A-Z guide to the key e-business terms and their meaning.

Adhocracy: A non-bureaucratic networked organization with a highly organic organizational design.

Affiliate marketing: Pioneered by the likes of Amazon and CDNow, anybody with a website can sign up with them as a sales affiliate and receive a commission (typically 5%-15%) for any sales that are channeled through the affiliate site.

Anoraknophobia: An exaggerated, irrational fear of computers and the Internet. It derives from 'anorak,' a term once used to describe a person with trainspotting tendencies but which has evolved to embrace people obsessed with technology.

Bricks and mortar: Companies that use traditional methods of selling and distributing products.

Browser: A software application that allows people to surf the web. Some of the most popular web browsers right now are Internet Explorer, Firefox and Safari.

Business process re-design: This involves changing both organizational structure and processes to ensure that future customer needs can be anticipated and fulfilled in the most cost-effective manner. This is generally known as business process re-design. It should not be confused with crude cost-cutting exercises (such as downsizing) although many organizations have used both approaches simultaneously, with the result that the value of process redesign has been permanently tarnished in the eyes of many managers.

Choiceboards: Interactive, online systems that let people design their own products from a menu of attributes, prices and delivery options.

Clusters: Critical masses of linked industries in one place that enjoy a high level of success in their particular field. Famous examples are Silicon Valley and Hollywood but clusters can be found everywhere.

According to Michael Porter, clusters can affect competition in three ways:

1. by increasing the productivity of companies based in the area
2. by driving the direction and speed of innovation in their field
3. by stimulating the formation of new businesses within the cluster.

Source: Derived from an article entitled 'Clusters and the New Economics of Competition' by Michael Porter, *Harvard Business Review*, November–December 1998.

Cluster geeking: The process by which devoted fans of anything from Dr Who to Lego bricks form internet communities to pursue their particular passion.

Communities of practice: Groups that form within an organization, typically of their own accord, where members are drawn to one other by a common set of needs that may be both professional and social. Compared to project teams, communities of practice are voluntary, longer-lived, have no specific deliverable, and are responsible only to themselves. Because they are free of formal strictures and hierarchy within an organization, they can be viewed as subversive.

Competitive advantage: John Kay, following in the footsteps of Michael Porter, defines competitive advantage as: 'The application of distinctive capability to a specific market place differentiating an organization from its competitors and allowing it to achieve above average returns in that market'.

Competitive convergence: This is what happens when companies are drawn towards imitation and homogeneity. The result is often static or declining prices and downward pressures on costs that compromise companies' ability to invest in the business in the long term.

Competitive intelligence: In a world of rapid technological change where new and sometimes surprising competitors can suddenly appear, a company's success will increasingly depend on how effectively it can gather, analyze and use information. According to Larry Kahaner, author of a book on the subject, companies that can turn raw information into powerful intelligence will 'build market share, launch new products, increase profits and destroy competitors'.

Confusion marketing: A process described by the UK Consumer Association as the way in which some businesses are seeking to deny customers the means of making an informed choice by swamping them with an excess of confusing price information. The intention is clear – to make price comparisons with rivals impossible in practical terms. The hope is that customers will give up in frustration and stay with, or move to, well-known companies or brands. Customers signing up for a mobile phone or obtaining a mortgage for a house purchase in the UK are facing confusion marketing tactics.

Core competents: The small number of people in an organization who are absolutely vital to that organization's success. Bill Gates has reflected that if 20 people were to leave Microsoft, the company would risk bankruptcy. In a study by the Corporate Leadership Council, a computer firm recognized 100 'core competents' out of 16,000 employees; a software company had 10 out of 11,000; and a transportation group deemed 20 of its 33,000 as really critical.

Customer Relationship Management (CRM): A set of techniques and approaches designed to a provide personalized service to customers and to increase customer loyalty. Increasingly viewed as a strategic issue, and one that typically requires technological support.

Cyberspace: Term originally coined by William Gibson in his book *Neuromancer*. Now generally used to describe the notional social arena we 'enter' when using computers to communicate.

Data marts: Scaled-down version of a data warehouse containing specific information of interest to a particular target group.

Data mining: The process of using advanced statistical tools to identify commercially useful patterns or relationships in databases.

Data warehouse: A database that can access all of a company's information.

Discontinuities: One-off changes in the market place that force radical change, e.g. Amazon's entry into the book market place.

Disintermediation: Buzzword for how the internet is cutting out the middlemen, enabling wholesalers/manufacturers to sell direct to the end user. Classic potential victims of disintermediation are estate agents and travel agents.

Domain name: Unique internet address used to identify a website, e.g. www.futurefilter.com

e-business: Using the internet or other electronic means to conduct business. The two most common models are B2C (Business-to-Consumer) and B2B (Business-to-Business). Partly due to news coverage given to high profile companies like Amazon, B2C is the better known model; on the other hand, B2B is growing faster than its more glamorous cousin.

e-by gum: A term to describe the quaint practice of sending a message via the traditional postal service using a sealed envelope.

e-commerce: Commercial activity conducted via the internet.

Ego surfing: Looking on the web for occurrences of one's own name.

e-lancers: independent contractors connected through personal computers and electronic networks. These electronically connected freelancers – e-lancers – join together into fluid and temporary networks to produce and sell goods and services.

e-tailing: Retail strategy based on selling and order processing via the web.

e-zines: The online equivalent of print-based newsletters and magazines.

Eyeballs: A measure of the number of visits made to a website.

Globalization: The integration of economic activity across national or regional boundaries, a process that is being accelerated by the impact of information technology.

Going dot.com: The trend that started in the US of leaving a well-paid job to join an internet organization.

HTML: Abbreviation for Hypertext Markup Language, a computer language, the one that most web pages are currently written in.

Infomediary: A company or individual that makes money by bridging the gap between companies' need for capture of detailed customer information and customers' desire for protection of such information from exploitation by companies.

Informate: Term coined by Harvard academic Shoshana Zuboff to describe the capacity for information technology to translate and make visible organizational processes, objects, behaviours and events.

Intellectual capital: Intellectual material – knowledge, information, intellectual property, experience – that can be put to use to create wealth. In a business context, the sum total of what employees in an organization know that gives it a competitive edge.

The Internot: Business executives or organizations that see no value from getting online. The term was devised by psychologist David Lewis, who also coined the phrase 'road rage" to describe when motoring frustration spills over. Research conducted by Lewis suggests that about half of all managers are Internots.

Intranet: A network designed to organize and share information that is accessible only by a specified group or organization.

ISP: Abbreviation for Internet Service Provider, the party that connects users to the internet.

Killer app: A new good or service that establishes an entirely new category and, by being first, dominates it, returning several hundred percent on the initial investment.

Knowledge management: A system, normally computer-based, to share information in a company with the goal of increasing levels of responsiveness and innovation. It may be *tacit* (inside the heads of individual staff-members, and possibly including personal experience, intuition, belief and values) or *explicit* (what has or can be written down, including technical specifications, procedures, training manuals, financial and management information).

Mass customization: Cost-efficient mass production of goods and services in lot sizes of one or just a few at a time as a matter of routine.

m-commerce: David Potter, Chairman of Psion, predicts that electronic commerce, today conducted largely via internet connected desk-tops will soon be overtaken by mobile (or m-) commerce using mobile phone technology.

Meme: An idea, behaviour, or skill that can be transferred from one person to another by imitation. Examples include the way in which we copy ideas, inventions, songs, catch-phrases and stories from one another. In a wired global economy, memes will have the capability of spreading at astonishing speeds.

Netiquette: A system of tacit codes encouraging members of the on-line community to uphold certain standards of behavior.

Net generation: A term coined by Don Tapscott to describe the first generation – now in their early teens to mid-twenties – to grow up surrounded by digital media.

New capitalism: A term coined by Robert Reich, former US Secretary for Labor, to characterize how the chief assets of new economy companies are intellectual assets rather than traditional assets like machinery, buildings etc.

One-to-one marketing: Customizing and personalizing a product or service to meet an individual's specific needs.

Out of the garage: A term for a young company that has just moved to its first real office.

Portal: Web page that serves as a start-point or central directory for a range of internet services.

Product overlap: This occurs when more than one generation of the same product is available simultaneously. For example, the original version of a piece of software may sell at a reduced price alongside the latest version at a higher price.

Push technology: The delivery of news and multimedia information via the world wide web to personal computers on people's desks. The Web is basically a 'pull' medium. Users decide what they want, point their browsers at the relevant website and then pull the designated pages back to their PCs.

Silver surfers: A term used to denote older members of the population who are comfortable 'surfing' the internet for information and services.

Spam: In a phrase, junk e-mail – unwanted messages sent to uninterested recipients.

Sticky content: The term refers to whether a website is alluring enough to 'catch' visitors as they go flying past. Until recently, most companies have concentrated their website efforts on increasing the flow of traffic to their site. Companies are now realizing that the emphasis needs to be less on attracting visitors on a one-off basis, and more on enticing visitors to stay, return again and even tell their friends.

Strategic Inflection Points: A term coined by Andy Grove to describe a moment in the life of a business when its fundamentals are about to change for better or worse.

10X force: Another term coined by Andy Grove to describe a super-competitive force that threatens the future of a business.

Technology Adoption Life Cycle: Model created by Geoffrey A. Moore to demonstrate the various points at which individuals will become involved with a technological innovation. Moore identifies five key groups that will become involved with any new technology at various stages of its life cycle:

1. Innovators: the technology enthusiasts.
2. Early adopters: the visionaries.
3. Early majority: the pragmatists.
4. Late majority: the conservatives.
5. Laggards: the sceptics.

Viral marketing: Releasing a catchy message, typically distributed online, with a view to the message reaching growing numbers of people, initially organically but then exponentially.

Virtual organization: An organizational form representing a loose combination of technology, expertise and networks.

VOIP: Short for Voice Over Internet Protocol, the means by which it is possible to make telephone calls using the internet rather than traditional landlines or mobile networks.

World wide web: The set of all information accessible using computers and networking.

Xanadu: Computer scientist Ted Nelson's planned global hypertext project, generally recognized as a forerunner of the web.

Zombies: dot.com companies that are on their last legs, waiting for their cash-burn rate to kill off the business.